GOD IS NEW EACH MOMENT

Edward Schillebeeckx

PROFESSOR EDWARD SCHILLEBEECKX
Foto De Gelderlander Pers, Nijmegen/Do Visser

GOD IS NEW EACH MOMENT

Edward Schillebeeckx

in conversation with Huub Oosterhuis and
Piet Hoogeveen

Translated by David Smith

continuum
LONDON • NEW YORK

Continuum

The Tower Building   15 East 26th Street
11 York Road   Suite 1703
London SE1 7NX   New York
                           NY 10010

First published in Great Britain, 1983 by T. & T. Clark Limited

Copyright © T. & T. Clark Ltd, 1983
This edition 2004

ISBN 0-8264-7701-1

Typeset by RefineCatch Limited, Bungay, Suffolk
Printed in Great Britain by Antony Rowe, Chippenham, Wiltshire

On 17 September 1982, His Royal Highness Prince Bernhard of the Netherlands handed the 1982 Erasmus Prize for Theology to Professor Edward Schillebeeckx in the presence of Her Majesty the Queen and many members of the Dutch Royal Family. This book was published to mark this occasion. Its publication was financed by a grant from the Praemium Erasmianum Foundation and by additional financial assistance given by Thijmgenootschap and the Flemish Province of the Dominican Order. Those who have subsidized the publication disclaim any responsibility for the contents of the book.

Contents

Foreword

When Edward Schillebeeckx was awarded the 1982 Erasmus Prize for Theology, several of his friends, including Paul Beugels, Henk Mattijsen and Dick de Zeeuw, asked me to collaborate in the composition of a book that would 'make his views and ideas more accessible to a wider circle of people'. The book was to be produced in time for it to be presented to him when he was given the Erasmus Prize on 17 September 1982.

I consulted Schillebeeckx' fellow-Dominican Jan Nieuwenhuis, his collaborator Nico Schreurs and the publisher Paul Brand, all of whom were very familiar with his work. I also consulted Schillebeeckx himself. The decision was made to prepare a book in dialogue form that would cover the main themes of his theology.

The conversations with Schillebeeckx took place between 1 March and 1 July 1982 in his study in the Albertinum, the Dominican monastery in Nijmegen.

I asked Piet Hoogeveen to take part in these conversations and he helped me to develop them. Piet Hoogeveen concluded his studies at the Catholic Faculty of Theology in Amsterdam in 1975 with a paper on the theology of K. H. Miskotte and he has since published a number of articles, including some on the Jewish thinker, Franz Rosenzweig.

One essential aspect of the kind of conversation consisting of questions and answers that forms the framework of this book is that the person questioned is, as it were, 'tempted' to say the same things again and again in different words and from different vantage-points. I have left statements that are at variance with each other in details as they are and I have not attempted to eliminate repetitions.

A great deal of what was said had, of course, to be adapted before the material recorded on tape could be made suitable for the printed page. I have, however, been most careful throughout to preserve Schillebeeckx' own distinctive mode of expressing himself and his own thought. He has himself checked everything and the published text has been authorised by him.

Huub Oosterhuis
July 1982

1

'That baby is God'

O. *When did you first hear about Jesus?*

S. The first thing I remember about my childhood — what came to the surface at once, as soon as you asked that question — is the enormous crib that we had at home every Christmas. It stood in one corner of the drawing-room on a large table. It was a kind of cabin made of brown paper to imitate rocks. It wasn't life-sized, but it was very big. There were a lot of figures, a whole caravanserai of camels, the three kings and, of course, the crib itself.

We still have bits of it at home. My sisters still put it up every Christmas.

O. *Where do they live?*

S. In Kortenberg, between Brussels and Louvain. I can still remember that Christmas scene very vividly because my mother had a fine alto voice and used to sing carols. We are all very sorry that we were never able to tape her voice. She sang wonderfully. I think that was why Christmas and the crib appealed so much to me as a child. And then, of course, there were all those human figures and, well, there is God — that baby is God! In so far as I remember it correctly, all that appealed to me!

O. *Did anyone tell you that — that baby is God?*

S. Yes, that was said. My father told me. He told the Christmas story to us children and told us what the figures represented — that is the black king Caspar and that baby is God.

As far as that was concerned, Father was our high-priest at home! I remember very well — when I was ordained, Mother said, before we began the meal that we had to celebrate the event: 'Now Edward must lead the prayers'. And my father brought his fist down on the table and said: 'Here at home I am the priest!'

O. *So your earliest memory is 'that baby is God'.*

S. Yes, that is my earliest memory.

O. *Faith began for you, then, with the telling of the Christmas story and you heard that 'proclamation of faith' from your father. How old were you then?*

S. I must have been four or five. My very earliest memory is of German soldiers in our garden in Kortenberg with a field kitchen. I have asked about this at home and was told it was in 1918 or 1919, that is, at the end of the First World War. I was born in 1914.

O. *What were your feelings when you heard those words: 'that baby is God'?*

S. They are difficult to describe. I experienced a feeling of awe.

O. *Did you still have that feeling years later, when you were ten or so?*

S. No, not at all. At that age I did not like the crib at all. Neither did my brothers and sisters!

O. *How did matters stand then with God?*

S. I served at Mass regularly from the age of six or seven onwards and then Christ was, as far as I was concerned, the host elevated after the consecration. I have no emotional reaction at all now at the moment of elevation, but I did then.

O. *What kind of emotions did you have?*

S. An emotion of 'that is God'.

O. *An emotion of security?*

S. No, rather an emotion of mystery. It was the same at the crib when I was younger. I had no emotion of security at the crib. We were always given severe warnings when we were around the crib: 'Look out! All that paper! It can easily be set alight!' Those warnings did not give us any sense of safety!

O. *You had vague emotions, then, when you were about ten or eleven and the host was elevated?*

S. Yes, that is right. But it was also because I served at Mass and looked at the host that the idea came to me: one day I shall be a priest.

O. *Why?*

S. Serving at Mass was something that was quite different from ordinary life. There was something sacral about it, something that was not present in ordinary life, but gave meaning to everyday experience. Well, I use the word 'sacral' now and of course that is not a word that a child would ever use! But I don't know a better one to describe what I experienced then.

O. *Did you perhaps want to be a member of the 'clergy' — to be a minister of that sacral element?*

S. No, that had nothing to do with it. It was above all a religious emotion that I experienced. In comparison with the other emotions that I felt, at home, at school, with my friends, in everyday life, this one had something special about it, something that attracted me especially.

O. *In the way that music can attract people?*

S. Yes, it was an emotion at that level. It was similar to the feelings I had for my father and mother. When I had done something wrong and the way those feelings would make up for it . . . I used to feel a world opening up before me that was much more profound than the world of everyday life. I had that feeling sometimes with my father and mother.

O. *And you could entrust yourself to that world? You had faith in it?*

S. Yes, that is right. You had faith in it. You could somehow believe in it. It gave you a kind of certainty, a kind of security. You did not feel a stranger in that world.

O. *What did your father do for a living?*

S. He worked as an accountant for the Public Records Office and must have prepared hundreds of bankruptcy cases for the courts. And reports! I have certainly got my habit of voluminous writing from him.

O. *How many children were there in your family?*

S. There were fourteen of us.

O. *Where were you in the family?*

S. I was the sixth.

O. *Did you live in harmony with each other at home?*

S. Oh yes, we did. We still have a family reunion twice a year! Even since my mother and father died. They are still the bond between us.

O. *Are all your brothers and sisters still alive?*

S. Two are dead. One died last year. The other — a doctor — died ten years ago in a car accident. That was terrible. He was on his rounds, driving along a country road. It was a sunken road. He was not driving fast — only about twenty miles an hour. The other driver was one of his closest friends. He was testing a Land Rover and was doing about a hundred miles an hour. He didn't see my brother. It was ten years ago.

O. *Have all fourteen of you remained Catholics?*

S. We have, but my bothers' and sisters' children haven't all continued to practise all the time, of course. But even they still belong to what we call the Schillebeeckx clan. My in-laws have several times talked about setting up a trade union of non-Schillebeeckx.

O. *Why did you say: they haven't all continued to practice all the time 'of course'?*

S. I was referring to a sociological trend that has been observed in many families. Oh, all my nephews and nieces still believe and they are still Catholic believers, but they are no longer automatically part of the same 'Church' tradition as their parents. They are no longer, as a matter of course, full, practising members of the Church as their parents were and are. On the other hand, however, they talk much more about religion than we did when we were young. But they don't take it for granted as we did. There is no need to place an unfavourable interpretation on this phenomenon — it has many positive aspects with regard to religion.

O. *Do your brothers and sisters read your books?*

S. They have them all, but I don't know whether they read them all. My father did — he read everything I wrote until he couldn't read any more. He read them with the help of a dictionary. My brothers and sisters read parts of them. But I don't think they have read my last two books, the big ones, on Jesus. To begin with, just after the Council, they all stood firmly behind me, but recently they have been less and less on my side. They think I am going too far.

O. *Politically too?*

S. Yes. They belong to the well-to-do middle class. They are doctors and engineers, for example, and people of that kind are not usually inclined towards the left wing.

O. *Let us go back to the time when you were ten. It was then that you had the vague feeling that you would become a priest. How did that develop?*

S. It would hardly be right to say that I was already conscious then of having a 'vocation'. I did, however, go to the Jesuit boarding-school in Turnhout when I was eleven and had been at the local school for several years, but that was partly to do with the fact that one of my brothers was a Jesuit. After his noviciate, he went to India and he is still there. He is seventy-six.

At the Jesuit school in Turnhout, I had first of all to follow two special preparatory courses, because I had not reached a sufficiently high standard at the local school. My brother was already a novice at that time in the Jesuit house in Arlon and he wrote letter after letter to me, recommending all kinds of typical Jesuit books. To begin with, these appealed to me — they were mostly, I remember, stories with a moral and religious tone about a very good boy called Tom Playfair. After he had sent me three of these adventure stories however, I told him that I no longer needed books of this kind. I got tired of them quickly enough.

O. *How open — or closed — was that Jesuit school when you were there?*

S. Turnhout was well known to be the strictest of all the Jesuit colleges at the time. The discipline was very firm and we had no contact at all with the outside world. I found myself becoming slowly but surely more and more opposed to the discipline. On the other hand, there were good personal contacts within the college itself. I am thinking here especially of one of my teachers, Seeldraayers. He had been brought up as a 'French' Belgian, but he was one of the great champions of the Flemish movement in our country. He made 'Flemish' Belgians of all of us at that time. He was very strict, but an excellent teacher. I had him for two years.

O. *What did he teach?*

S. Everything. Greek. Latin. Not religion, though. He was rather out on a limb in the Jesuit community. We found him fascinating.

O. *Did he help you to clarify that vague feeling of 'vocation' in your own mind?*

S. Yes, he set my thoughts in order. He had an entirely rational turn of mind.

O. *What objections did you yourself have to this vocation?*

S. I had no objections at all. It was still very vague indeed. It was not until I was in the fifth form at school that the feeling became much clearer and I definitely wanted to become a Jesuit.

O. *You were fifteen or sixteen at the time, I suppose?*

S. Fifteen. I wanted to become a Jesuit and go to India. Not so much in order to be a missionary as to study Hinduism and Buddhism. My brother suggested I should read a book by Wallace about an Indian convert to Christianity. I still have the notes I took when I read it. It fascinated me and I went on to read other books about Hinduism and Buddhism. I wanted to make a comparative study of Christianity and Buddhism.

O. *But how did you, as a boy of fifteen, come to compare Christianity with the religions of India?*

S. Wallace's book led me to it.

O. *What did Christianity mean to you at that time?*

S. It was a doctrine, of course.

O. *With Jesus at the centre?*

S. With God as the Trinity at the centre too. I am bound to say that we fifteen-year-old boys knew more about that then than first-year theology students know now at Nijmegen University. The catechism was drummed into our heads at school in those days.

O. *Did you have an apologetical purpose when you set out to compare Christianity and the Eastern religions?*

S. My aim was certainly not exclusively apologetical. What struck me above all were the many parallels between the Trinity in Christian teaching and similar data, such as the Trimurti with Brahma, Vishnu and Shiva in Hinduism.

O. *Had that Christian Trinity any connection at all with your own world as a* *fifteen-year-old boy? Were you conscious, for example, of any links between God the Father and your own father?*

S. No, I wasn't. The Trinity was simply a 'doctrine' and had nothing to do with my active or emotional life. In the same way, I also regarded the Trimurti in Hinduism simply as a doctrine.

O. *You found it intellectually fascinating?*

S. Yes, I did.

O. *Did you read much literature at the Jesuit college? Greek and Latin authors, of course . . .*

S. Yes, we did classical literature, but not much attention was paid to its aesthetic aspect. We were not very concerned with whether Homer's Greek was beautiful or not, for example. The emphasis was entirely phiological. I was very good at Greek when I was at school. I could even give an improvized talk to the class in Greek — the language was so firmly drummed into us! I can hardly read a word of it now!

But my main interest was in sociological books. I used to read them during the holidays.

O. *Sociology?*

S. Well, at that time, of course, they were books about social questions. That interest was first aroused in me by Father de Wit, who taught at the school and was deeply committed to social questions. We got on very well with each other.

It was the practice at the time in our boarding-school to bring in the riff-raff of Turnhout — boys of twelve or thirteen — from the streets and give them clothes and so on. In exchange for clothes and food, they had to make our beds, serve us at table and so on. Father de Wit thought that this wasn't good enough as a form of social work and he got me to give them religious instruction. We produced a little magazine for them too.

O. *What was that called?*

S. *Kent Mervel* — an odd name, but it was a slogan that Father Seeldraayers used to use. It is Irish, I think. I can't remember what it means! I think it must have had something to do with the movement for Irish freedom that was so prominent at the time. Seeldraayers used to talk a lot about that. When those words came back to me later in life, I thought they were Hungarian. There were lost of Hungarian children in Belgium in those years. I remember we had a Hungarian child with us at home. I suppose the two memories must have become confused with each other.

O. *So you were socially committed?*

S. Yes, I was, thanks to Father de Wit. I became more intellectually committed, not only socially of course, under the influence of Father Seeldraayers.

O. *When did you become really convinced that you wanted to be a priest?*

S. I wanted to go to India until I went into the first year of the sixth form at school.

O. *As a priest?*

S. Oh yes, that went without saying. But I wanted to be a priest in India. There are several letters at home that I wrote then, it is quite amusing — I drew a boat, the boat that would take me to India and fulfil my youthful expectations! One letter has a drawing of a bicycle. I was going to use a bike to get me around in India.

When I was in the sixth form, though, I began to reflect seriously about what I wanted to do. I remember I had a serious quarrel with Father de Wit. He found me talking to another boy during a study period. I claimed that it was quite reasonable to talk because the other boy was 'stuck'. But de Wit said: 'It is not allowed on principle'. 'The principle doesn't mean anything to me', I retorted. 'That boy needed me.' Later, de Wit said to me: 'You were right. But principles take precedence.' I didn't like that at all, especially in someone whom I liked and admired personally.

We had vocation retreats in the sixth form. The whole class would go to a retreat house and well-known preachers would be invited to conduct the retreats. The Jesuits had a large number of excellent preachers and so many of the boys became Jesuits. But it was really a form of indoctrination in the guise of objectivity. They were in fact fishing for vocations. Hoping to make a catch, that's what it was. In my case, it had precisely the opposite effect. I became opposed to the Jesuits. And I realised that I was more concerned with India than with becoming a Jesuit.

O. *So it was when you were on retreat that you saw that becoming a Jesuit was not the main thing?*

S. Yes, that's right. And I remember thinking — and here you have evidence, I suppose, of my very rational approach to things — I must systematically go through biographies of Ignatius, Dominic, Francis and Benedict. Then, when I have studied their lives, I will make a choice and join the followers of one of them.

When I had finished my course of reading, I had no doubt. The one who appealed to me most was Dominic. I think it was a book by Clérissac on *L'Esprit de Saint Dominique* that influenced me most.

O. *What attracted you particularly in Dominic?*

S. A combination of intellect and something universal and harmonious. I was struck by the delicate balance between religion on the one hand and humanity and being in and with the world on the other.

O. *You were not attracted by the Jesuit spirit of combat, their competitiveness, their emphasis on achievement and on achieving more than others?*

S. No, I wasn't. The Dominicans stressed the priority of grace and wanted to 'let God be God'.

O. *Did you know any Dominicans when you made your decision?*

S. No, I didn't. I had known the Jesuits for eight years, but I had never seen a Dominican in my life. There were none in Turnhout. So, when I was nineteen, I went in search of them. I found out that they had a noviciate in Ghent. The prior there was Father Matthijs and he invited me to spend a week in Ghent during the summer holiday. He enclosed a reproduction of a fresco showing Dominic embracing Francis — it was by Fra Angelico, I think — in his letter to me and I well remember how deeply affected I was by this very emotional picture.

O. *You were moved by the warmth and harmony?*

S. Yes. It radiated warmth. Friendships were not allowed in the Jesuit houses and anything that was even remotely connected with emotion was squashed at once. Then suddenly a Dominican I didn't even know sent me a picture depicting human warmth! It had an enormous effect on me. I've still got that picture.

I went to Ghent and my visit was a real revelation for me. Philosophy was taught there with a great deal of attention to the doctrine of God. The Dominican theological college was at Louvain at that time and their theology was all done with social questions in mind. The combination of the two was exactly what I was looking for.

O. *Do you think your preference for the Dominicans had anything to do with the harmony that you experienced at home? Did you find that their way of life was a continuation of the life that you had led with your parents?*

S. Yes, I did. As a novice, I was treated as an equal and that was how I had been treated at home. Father and Mother were very demanding, but they were never strict. If we had tried something on, for example, Father used to come up to our room at night-time and talk about it. We were always given a chance to defend ourselves. I suppose that was quite exceptional in those days. When I think back to when I was a boy, I can only recall good things.

O. *Did you see joining the Dominicans as a vocation?*

S. Yes.

O. *What was your attitude towards the decision to remain unmarried?*

S. It wasn't a conscious decision. I wanted to become a Dominican and that meant entering a monastery and, as a consequence, being celibate.

O. *What did you think at that time about a life without sexuality?*

S. We just didn't think about it. At the Jesuit boarding-school, you simply had to curb everything that had to do with sexuality or you couldn't become a priest. In that sense, of course, sexuality had a part to play in our lives. But I don't remember consciously choosing to be celibate. I might even say, I suppose, that I am not personally committed to it. Later, of course, as a theologian, I have certainly reflected about celibacy and tried to find the meaning of it.

O. *What meaning did you give to it?*

S. I have written about celibacy three times, I think. The last time was in 1980 in my book on office in the Church, which was published in the United States as *Ministry*. Before that, there was an article in the *Tijdschrift voor Theologie* in 1965 and in 1966 there was my little book *Het ambtsceli-baat in de branding*. In that article and that little book that I wrote in the nineteen-sixties, I dealt especially with celibacy as a sign. My argument was that it was precisely in its negativity, its detachment, that celibacy made the gratuitous nature of grace visible. I based my ideas very largely on Karl Rahner's studies. In my most recent book, however, I have revised that view of celibacy. It is no longer clear how it is possible for you to be obliged to opt for the celibate life in order to become a priest, unless you do it in the way that everyone is able to do it — you do not want to commit yourself to a family, for example, or you may prefer to opt for your work. This has, of course, very little to do with sexuality as such. You can choose to be 'free', for example. That played a part in my case, I think, when I became a religious. But it is different from opting for sexual continence.

O. *Have there never been times in your life when you regretted having remained unmarried?*

S. I have had a lot of contact with young families in the last ten years or so — the families of my brothers' and sisters' children. I can see that possibilities are open to them that I have never made use of. But no, I have no regrets. Look at it from the other point of view: if I had been married, I would have not written so many books. But, of course, I would also have written quite differently from the way in which I write now as a celibate.

O. *Can you define that more precisely?*

S. When I am with married people, I have the feeling that they ask different questions. Even their religious questions are different. In the long run, because of my association with them, I have also come to ask different questions. Here in the Albertinum in Nijmegen, where I live, the total separation between the monastic life and life in the world no longer exists. In the past, after your training, you only met women in the confessional. Now the situation is quite different. Less intense. More open and healthier. Affectionate relationships with people influence your theology, of course. I think my two Jesus books would have been quite different if I had been married. They might have had greater depth. But I could not have written many of my books. If I had, it would have had a very damaging effect on my wife and children. It is a bit late to say it now, of course, but I have always worked very long hours — day and night, in fact.

O. *Would you like to meet a woman now, someone who might be a partner in life?*

S. No, I would no longer want to marry now or cohabit with anyone. I have very intimate and authentic friendships with people of both sexes, although I experience them as a celibate.

O. *Do you feel that they are complete relationships?*

S. I have no sense of lack in my life as far as that is concerned.

O. *You said just now that you have always worked day and night. You have written books. Was that your task in life?*

S. Looking back at my life, I would say: yes, that was my task. But I didn't set out with that preconceived intention and I didn't really aim to write books and articles. It was simply that writing was involved in my life and work. Even when I was a student, I sometimes used to write an entire number of the Dominican students' paper, *Biekorf*. And as soon as I had finished my studies, I began writing articles straightaway.

O. *You joined the Dominicans, you studied philosophy and theology and you were ordained priest.*

S. Yes, I was ordained in 1941.

O. *Did you know then that you would spend the rest of your life as a theologian?*

S. To begin with, I wanted to be a philosopher. I studied philosophy for three years in Ghent. Then I had to do my military service. But because I was able to get exemption from almost everything through the chaplain, I managed to continue with my philosophical studies. After the first-aid lesson, I was able to spend the whole day reading Kant. I studied a great deal of sociology and psychology too during that period. And although I knew nothing about Marxism, I was preoccupied with the question as to what governed history. Was it ideas or economics? When I was doing theology at Louvain, I went on doing philosophy on my own for another two years. Theology — and theology at Louvain in those days was Thomas Aquinas' *Summa Theologiae* — meant nothing to me. When De Petter, who was our master of studies then, heard how little I cared for theology, he had me up on the carpet and told me: 'That is quite wrong. You must really try to work your way into theology. If the *Summa* doesn't mean anything to you, begin with Karl Adam.'

O. *What was he?*

S. He taught dogmatic theology in the Catholic Faculty at Tübingen during the first half of this century. He wrote books that were read by people who had nothing to do with universities. Two very well known books that were published in the nineteen-twenties were *Christ our*

Brother and *The Spirit of Catholicism*. Before the Second World War, Karl Adam renewed Catholic theology by following a course that was different from neo-scholastic rationalism. He was above all inspired by the Latin Fathers of the Church and especially by Augustine.

O. *You never hear of him now.*

S. No, that's true and it's probably because he defended Nazism during the war. But he had a very deep influence on theology at the time.

O. *What were his most important themes?*

S. He discussed in great detail the essence of Christian teaching. He analysed and expounded all the dogmas of the Church from the Trinity to the Immaculate Conception and didn't use a single scholastic term in all his work. That appealed to me enormously.

O. *Did he found a school of theology? Did he, for instance, have any influence on Frits van der Meer's* Catechism, *which is still an impressive book?*

S. I am certain of it. Everyone read Karl Adam during the years that preceded the Second World War.

O. *But his theology did not incorporate any of the findings of biblical research?*

S. Oh yes, it did. He was one of the first Catholic theologians to make use of them. But Catholic exegesis did not have much to offer in those days and Catholics did not read the work of Protestant exegetes. They only began to do that after the war. Karl Adam, though, studied the Bible. There are splendid pages in his books on the 'psychology of Jesus', containing elements of concern for the *man* Jesus that was to develop later.

O. *Why were you more drawn to philosophy than to theology?*

S. Theology was at that time mainly playing with concepts. In philosophy, on the other hand, we were concerned with humanity. De Petter, who taught me philosophy, emphasised that very strongly. Sociology and psychology played a very important part in his philosophy, which was really a philosophical anthropology. This was very much in accordance with my own interests at the time. At the same time, De Petter's philosophy was strongly orientated towards theological questions. He was always asking how you could approach God from the vantage-point of human thought. The theology that was taught at Louvain was, however, not entirely in keeping with this. When I read Karl Adam's books,

13

however, I began to realise that it was certainly possible to form a solid link between theology and philosophy, with its references to the religious question. As soon as I had discovered that possibility, I began to study theology in a really personal way, stimulated especially by articles written by Rousselot on the 'eyes of faith'. Rousselot genuinely re-discovered the *lumen fidei* — the 'light of faith' — in those articles and gave a fresh impetus to the aspect of human experience in faith. That aspect had become almost entirely lost in post-Tridentine Catholic theology.

O. *I remember De Petter's article on 'implicit intuition' when I was studying myself with the Jesuits. Did that article make an impression on you?*

S. That article was published in 1939. When I was studying with De Petter, that was before 1939, he was not using that term, although he was obviously moving in that direction. He gave me the task, in my third year of philosophy, that is, between 1937 and 1938, of finding out the best ways of overcoming conceptuality. I remember I made an analysis of the relationship between question and answer in my essay and looked in that direction for the non-conceptual element in reason.

O. *I suppose you mean the intuitive, contemplative element?*

S. Yes. In that article he wrote in 1939, De Petter shows that intuition forms an essential part of the intellect. It is our spiritual link with the things around us. A direct experience of those things and, in it, an experience of the meaning of all that. But that intuitive element is implicit — De Petter lays great stress on this. The link, that direct experience of the totality of everything, has still to be understood and explicitated. But the fact that this is possible has its origin in that implicit, contemplative element. In my opinion, however, all this points too much in the direction of idealism. I certainly no longer agree completely with De Petter in this.

O. *What attracted me so much in De Petter's article on 'implicit intuition' was the idea that, in your experience of yourself as living, thinking and feeling there is an indication and even the beginning of an experience of totality and of feeling yourself to be linked to everything. That experience of being connected seems to me to be one of the fundamental experiences of all religions.*

S. Yes, De Petter was also convinced of this. But, in our modern world, with its great diversity of philosophies and views of life, it is no longer possible to accept as your point of departure a single total meaning and regard that as the source of separate experiences of meaning. All the same, although I don't go along entirely with him now, I owe a great deal to De Petter, mainly because he gave a relative value to theology as a system of concepts. That was the great and really significant change both for him and for me. I have never deviated from that conviction.

O. *So De Petter insisted that there should be room for human experience within theology?*

S. Yes. You have to take that experience as your point of departure. To begin with, that concept — 'experience' — was hardly a clearly defined theme in my work — it was only much later that I presented it systematically — but even when I was a student I always wanted to go back to concrete experience. Later I knew with certainty that 'the concept' was not everything. Shortly after the war, when I was studying in Paris, I encountered the same tendency — back to concrete sources! *Ressourcement!* At that time, of course, that meant a study of mediaeval sources from the Carolingian period up to the time of Thomas Aquinas. My feeling for history developed a great deal when I was in Paris.

H. *Back to concrete experience. Did that mean for you first and foremost back to historical experience?*

S. Yes, certainly. Back to the early sources. Back to the Church Fathers and back to biblical experience, although that came later. It happened precisely the other way round with the Protestants — they began by returning to biblical experience. My development in this direction can be traced quite easily in the book that I published in 1952, *De sacramentele heilseconomie*. I began with Thomas Aquinas and went back from him to the Church Fathers and then forward to the problems of today. There was hardly any biblical exegesis at all in that book. What little there was served the purpose of illustration.

O. *You were employed in your order in the training of priests. What type of priest had you in mind? Did you have any form of 'spirituality' for priests in your training?*

S. I began teaching theology in 1947 and I lived in two different worlds. On the one hand, I was responsible for all the courses in dogmatic theology. In four years, I taught everything, from the theology of creation to eschatology. I did that two-and-a-half times, that is, for ten years. Until 1957, when I was appointed to Nijmegen University. That was one world

— the world of study. On the other hand, I was also the students' *magister spiritualis*. In other words, I had to give spiritual guidance to sixty students.

I formed a religious community with those students and in that community I functioned not so much as a 'master' as as an elder brother. So I did away with most of the rules, since these had been the cause of many of the conflicts between the students and the superior and the other fathers, including De Petter, who had been my predecessor as *magister* in Louvain. He was in fact a very strict 'master' and made the students write an account every week of their experiences, which he regularly read. I put an end to that practice at once. Poor De Petter! He saw all his ideals suddenly swept aside by a snotty-nosed boy! The conflicts in my life haven't simply been limited to recent years! But the training of priests in Louvain was more progressive then than it was in Nijmegen. When I came here in 1957, I thought I had gone back into the Middle Ages!

H. *In the religious community that you formed with your students, I imagine prayer played an important part. Was there an interplay between prayer and social action at that time?*

S. No, there was no direct interaction between the two. I was deeply interested in social matters and that interest dated from the time that I was at the Jesuit school in Turnhout. It was also greatly strengthened by my contacts with the worker-priests when I was in Paris. That was a very profound experience for me and those ideas were all present in the lectures I gave. Some students were sufficiently influenced by them to go further in that direction. I think I more or less drove them to it.

O. *Why did you drive them in that direction?*

S. Firstly because of my own social commitment and secondly because there were hardly any priests or religious leaders at all in working-class environments. That was the basic idea of the *présence au monde*. The term originated with Lacordaire, of course, but it was developed by Chenu, whom I had got to know in Paris.

H. *What did Chenu mean to you?*

S. He probably did more than anyone else to inspire my theological thinking and he influenced not just by what he said, but by his whole personality. He is eighty-six now and he is still inspiring! When you meet him, you feel as though a fragment of the power of nature itself is coming towards you, a prophet who lives in the future, but who is able to give you hope for the present from his understanding of the future and for whom freedom is the beginning and the end of everything and conditions everything. For me he was the embodiment of the Dominican ideal as I wanted to experience it. He wrote a little book on the theology of the Dominican school in Paris, Le Saulchoir, which was condemned by Rome in 1941, inspired me enormously, as did his theological training of the worker-priests. When he was eighty, he wrote: 'I always begin by listening — opening all my ears'. In fact, he always spoke as though he had more than just two ears. 'I want to listen to people's experience', he used to say, 'and only then do I apply critical analysis'.

Chenu is also the man who introduced the phrase 'the signs of the times' into theology. He was never a systematic theologian. He was always concerned with the world and much less interested in problems within the Church or churches. Even before he had fully developed as a theologian, he was always opposed to ideology. I myself learned from Chenu, after his teaching had been condemned, how to carry on when you are under suspicion in Rome. Even before there was any liberation theology, he defined the Church as a 'Church of the poor and oppressed' and the 'messianic community of the poor'.

During the Second Vatican Council, he was on the way to Saint Peter's one day and, feeling hot and tired, sat down by Bernini's column. An Italian girl came past him and looked at the old man in his white habit and saw that he was sweating. She went on, but came back a little later and put a handkerchief soaked in eau de cologne on his forehead. He at once turned towards her and embraced her! That was absolutely characteristic of Chenu!

H. *What did that really mean: 'being present in the world'?*

S. It meant you had to go and live, as a priest, someone who had been trained in religion, among the people and especially among working-class people. You did not have to talk about God and the Church, but just be there, among people, in the hope that they would become aware of something — a deeper mystery — because of your Christian praxis, your way of life. The strategy of being present in the world was to awaken in others the religious question and to do that by your way of life.

A very important part in that movement was played by Rosier's book, *I Sought God's Absence*. Rosier, a Carmelite, showed quite clearly that the sense of religion had not entirely disappeared in the secularised environment in which the working classes lived. It was still very much present,

17

although it was hidden. We thought we could help to set that hidden religiosity free by our strategy of 'being present in the world'.

I discussed these themes in great detail in the lectures I gave to my students. One main theme, which was also the title of a whole series of lectures, was *Tu es deus absconditus* — 'You are a hidden God'. In contact with God you come up against a brick wall. You enter the dark night. And prayer is just holding on, a feat of endurance. A little while ago I re-read some of those lectures. They are full of bits of Latin — verses of the psalms, which we knew by heart in Latin in those days. That makes rather a strange impression nowadays, but a lot of it is quite easily recognisable.

O. *You were, I suppose, brought into contact with the Bible through the liturgy, your prayer together in choir?*

S. Yes, we became familiar with the Bible and especially with the psalms, of course, in the liturgy and in communal prayer. Not in study.

O. *Did you also read René Voillaume's books in the nineteen-fifties in Louvain, like the one in which he went into the spirituality of Charles de Foucauld and used it as a source of inspiration? Was that spirituality very close to that of the worker-priests?*

S. I read all those books and even bought them for my students, who devoured them. My only real criticism of them was that they neglected the aspect of reflection and study.

O. *They were really testimonies — letters. Spirituality in action.*

S. That's right. But I have always believed very firmly that theological reflection must follow praxis. If it doesn't, praxis becomes too vague.

H. *How did you manage to discover a connection between theological reflection and the 'praxis' of the worker-priests?*

S. I could see that there were many students at that time who wanted to be worker-priests, so I said: that's fine and the best part that I can play in this as a theologian is to reflect about that praxis. Looking back at the whole movement now — it all took place in the nineteen-fifties — I can see that we were unconsciously experimenting with a model that was further elaborated later into the liberation theology. Praxis came first and theology was the second step. In theological reflection, you try to ascertain the degree of authenticity in that praxis, as seen from the vantage-point of faith.

O. *Has that continued to be the model for your theology?*

S. Yes, it has. We really tested it thoroughly at that time. We left with two coach-loads of students for the East German frontier — that was after quite a serious quarrel with the superior, who didn't like the idea at all. I knew a very progressive German pastor — he is vicar-general now in Bonn and just as progressive as ever. Jansen, that's his name. At that time, he was working for the refugees. As soon as he told me he needed a reception centre, I said: good, I will bring my students and we'll build a centre for you. We did in fact go there in the long vacation. We did physical work during the day and in the evenings I and Pastor Jansen led 'theological reflection'. We had very wide-ranging theological discussions and that and the physical work formed us into a very close community. Afterwards, the students described their experiences and I tried to evaluate them theologically. My experience in Germany that year convinced me that quite small communities should be set up in the future for Dominicans.

O. *Did that in fact happen?*

S. Several small groups were formed and a beginning was made. There was one, consisting of six people, in Genk. But in the long run, the idea was more or less squashed by the Dominican establishment. Most of the groups gradually disappeared as first one, then another member was transferred by someone in authority. One of my students is still a tram conductor! He is a bit of a mystic, but a mystic with a conductor's cap on his head.

2

'The Story of a Living One'

O. *You have elaborated your ideas about Jesus in your most recent books. When did you first begin, as a theologian, to approach the figure of Jesus?*

S. When I was in Louvain. I taught Christology there, real dogmatic theology, in other words. But as the students' spiritual director I also had to give a number of lectures on spirituality and I took as my point of departure in those lectures the man Jesus, in whom what God really means for us is made clear to us. Those lectures had an influence on the dogmatic theology that I was teaching, with the result that, in my Christology, I took Jesus as God as my point of departure, but at the same time I also tried to find a connection with Thomas Aquinas' disputed term *persona humana divinae naturae* — 'a human person of divine nature'. It was at that time that I wrote my first study of the New Testament. It was not very scientific, but it was to some extent quite critical. In it, I asked the question: Who is Jesus in the New Testament? But if I compare what I was doing then with the way I tackle the subject now . . .!

In Louvain at that time, exegesis was based on Kittel — the famous German dictionary of the New Testamant. This was in itself a sign of real progress. It went much further than the kind of exegesis that was normally practised in Catholic schools of theology in those days. But, on the other hand, everything that departed in Kittel from the traditional Catholic exegesis was carefully eliminated. Exegesis had to provide proofs for dogma! I had to teach Christology for the second time in Louvain in 1955 and I made a point of studying the whole of modern Christology.

O. *Was there any Roman Catholic Christology that could be called modern at that time?*

S. Insofar as there was any, it had been written by Franciscan theologians, neo-scholastics for the most part. I forget their names now. But, following their centuries-old tradition of spirituality, they gave great emphasis to the humanity of Jesus. I continued along that path. When I came to Nijmegen in 1957, I began with eschatology and an analysis of theological methods.

I did not do Christology again until 1969 and then I said: I have got to become completely familiar with the whole of modern exegesis before I even begin. So I spent three or four years doing nothing else but study exegetes. That was all preparatory work before I began to write *Jesus, an Experiment in Christology.*

O. *The title of that book in Dutch, not in English, was a brilliant discovery:* Jesus, the Story of a Living. *It was open-ended in Dutch: 'a living', but it wouldn't go into English. It had a classical flavour and sounded like a liturgical formula, but at the same time it was quite up-to-date.*

S. Yes, that title was a sure-fire hit! Seen from the purely commercial point of view, I think it was the title rather then the book itself that attracted many people. I wasn't able to find such a good title for the second volume. *Christ, the Christian Experience in the Modern World — Justice and Love* in Dutch — both are much less concrete. On the other hand, there is much more material in that book for preachers and discussion groups. But it hasn't sold so well. It is too long, I admit. But I think that the title also puts people off.

O. *What was your aim in writing the Jesus book?*

S. My main intention was to dissociate the story of Jesus from all that dogmatic theology and to go back to that man, Jesus of Nazareth, who appeared in that place and at that time. And then to follow the whole of that way — what he said and did and how his apostles reacted to what he said and did and above all how they reacted to his death on the cross.

O. *You wanted to go back to the Jesus of history, in other words.*

S. Yes. That was for me the new approach.

H. *What is the difference between your search for the 'Jesus of history' and the nineteenth-century 'quest for the historical Jesus'?*

S. The historical critical method employed in that quest was intended to make those who read the Bible more critical of tradition. The rational attitude challenged the authority of tradition. The Bible was in this way dissociated from its inner link with the community of the Church and given an objective value by critical scientific methods. Scholars believed they could protect the different nature of the text of the Bible in this way from a subjective approach. But this very historical critical approach lead to a break in the pre-critical approach of tradition. The original unity that existed between the text and the reader, between the Bible and the community of the Church, was broken and this led to the subject and the object becoming separated. This kind of opposition between subject and object is in fact a power-structure. The object is passive, but the subject is active and so the present situation of the subject — the exegete — threatens to become normative with regard to the object, the text.

O. *Let me try to summarize what you have been saying. Exegetes thought they could protect the distinctive character of the text of the Bible from autonomous subjectivity, but they did not succeed in avoiding the danger that they wanted to prevent. The liberal critical exegetes did in fact impose their own subjective and historically conditioned norms on the text, which was 'passive' and could not, as it were, defend itself, and they were not really aware of their position of power in this respect. Is that a correct summary?*

S. Yes, it is. We can see, then, how those liberal critical exegetes projected their own liberal nineteenth-century ideals into Jesus. I have used a historical critical method as well, but I have tried, as it were in a kind of 'second innocence', to restore the original inner link that existed between the Bible and the community of believers.

The liberal exegesis of the Bible had no band of followers gathered from far and wide to whom it could appeal — it was only relevant for the in-group of liberal exegetes themselves. And even though it began as a criticism of dogmatism and orthodoxy in the Church, it ended by confirming the social *status quo*. It didn't lead to emancipation and it didn't stimulate liberation.

I hope, with my critical approach to the 'Jesus of history' to clear the way for a new interplay between the text and the reader of the Bible, so that the reader is stimulated by the text to become personally and socially emancipated and liberated. The 'religious result' of an approach of this kind is fundamentally different from that of the nineteenth-century 'quest for the historical Jesus'.

H. *So you are really fundamentally concerned with keeping the link between the Bible and the community of believers as close as possible?*

S. Yes, I am. I studied the whole field of scientific exegesis for fifteen years, I think, before completing *Jesus* and during that time I noticed that academic exegetes put different questions to the Bible from those that ordinary believers have been hearing read out of the Bible or have themselves read in the Bible. An enormous gulf has developed between believers and academic exegetes. I now realise it is just no longer possible to remain in that state of 'first innocence' and not to move on from that direct link. Academic exegesis is quite necessary, even for the community of believers. The two ought to be much more closely in tune with each other. At the present stage of things, however, the ordinary Christian cannot do anything with the results of scientific exegesis and the exegete cannot answer the questions asked by the ordinary Christian.

O. *Let me ask one question that might be put by the community of ordinary believers: What is the key-word in the story of Jesus? What is he really concerned with?*

S. In my study of the Bible and biblical exegesis since leaving Louvain, it has become quite clear to me — he is concerned with the 'kingdom of God'. That is the key-word — the kingdom. What is expressed in it is that God's affair is man's affair. God identifies himself with man's affair. He is concerned with oppressed and enslaved man. He is the God of the poor. His kingdom is wherever justice is done to those who have been deprived of their rights. Jesus is concerned with that kingdom. It is obvious from all his words, insofar as we can reconstruct them, that he stands up for the oppressed. In doing that, he also proclaims a new concept of God. He proclaims the God of Israel, but at the same time he wants that original concept of God — the idea that God is a 'God of the poor' — to be able to function in a new way in society. The original Old Testament concept of God in the long run functioned to the disadvantage of the poor. It is quite clear from everything in the story of Jesus that he was opposed to the malfunction of the Jewish concept of God.

O. *And in that respect, he was in the tradition of Amos and other Old Testament prophets.*

S. Yes, he is the classical prophetic tradition. He also called himself a prophet. He was even 'more than a prophet'. He said that of himself and it is one of his *ipsissima verba*, one of his very own words. He knows that about himself. It is part of his own consciousness of himself. He is the 'eschatological' prophet, the ultimate prophet, proclaiming the gospel to the poor. He sees himself as the last prophet for Israel. He wanted to bring Israel together, bring the people back to their own sources, their own roots. He is very close indeed to the outline of the eschatological prophet provided by Isaiah.

As a prophet, he says nothing that is new. Even the commandment to love our enemies can be found in the Old Testament. The 'whole law', Jesus tells us, depends on that commandment to love. But then, in the story of the rich young man who had kept all the commandments, who had, in other words, kept the 'whole law', Jesus says: 'One thing you still lack. Sell all that you have and distribute it to the poor'. The radical nature of that statement in Luke 18 is something that I have never encountered in the classical prophetic tradition of the Old Testament. It is, I think, unique.

O. *You think, then, that it is unique, like Peter's statement about him in the Acts of the Apostles (4:10): 'There is salvation in no one else'. You began* Jesus *by quoting that text. Don't you find them difficult, those words 'in no one else'?*

S. The unique character of Jesus is, I admit, an enormous problem, especially when this is expressed, as it is in the Acts of the Apostles, in an exclusive way: 'There is no salvation, except in the name of Jesus'. I object to this, precisely because it is formulated in such an exclusive way. At the same time, I subject my critical attitude to the authority of the Judaeo-Christian tradition.

I admit that a centuries-old tradition may be very wide of the mark. I do not regard that tradition as a norm because it has been formulated in precisely that way from the beginning until the present time. It is quite possible that something has been expressed in a certain way in complete continuity, but that we now recognize, because our world-image or our view of man is different or because our needs as a community of believers have changed, that it can also be expressed differently. This applies particularly to the structures of the Church, of course. Even if we had had the same structures from New Testament times until the present day, this does not in any sense mean that those structures would form part of the 'unchangeable nature' of the Church. The 'it was so from the beginning' cannot be identified with the 'essence' of the Church. Continuity from the beginning may also have non-theological causes. It may, for example, have purely social and historical causes. In my view, this is clearly the case in the exclusion of women from office in the Church. The unique character of Jesus, however, in the transcendent sense of that word, is confessed in the whole of the Judaeo-Christian tradition. And, unless counter-arguments are put forward which are sufficiently convincing to make me change my mind, then I too will continue to have difficulties with that exclusive formulation.

O. *Jesus of Nazareth evoked the messianic vision of the liberation of the poor and the oppressed, the vision of the kingdom of God, in other words and let us see it with the eyes of our heart and our conscience. He was the man who presented us with that vision, the prophet, and even now, centuries later, there are many people who try to live in the light of that inspiration. Hasn't enough been said about this already?*

S. You could say that Jesus evoked a vision of the kingdom of God and we live from it. If you do that consistently, you are doing a great deal. I do not want to minimalise that, but I have certain questions to ask about that kind of formulation, because there have been various people in history who have been like that — prophets who have evoked the vision of liberation, the vision of the kingdom of God.

How, then, do you explain the fact that this particular man, Jesus, living in an out-of-the-way part of the Middle East, was able to launch a great movement such as Christianity, whereas his contemporary, John the Baptist, who proclaimed a similar message and had a very similar ideal in mind, disappeared, together with his whole movement, which was, it should not be forgotten, a very important one at the time? The historical fact of the Jesus movement — well, it can, of course, be understood in a purely horizontal way. But the New Testament — and not just Paul — has more to say than that. We only have to think again of the Acts of the Apostles. Peter says: 'There is no other name under heaven given among men by which we must be saved' — no other name other than that of Jesus of Nazareth. That definitive quality in Jesus — that is the great Christological problem.

O. *Bhagwan's followers talk in very much the same way about Bhagwan. For them, he is the definitive master, the only master. And when he was converted to a completely different view of life, the socialist way, the poet Herman Gorter also began to talk in the same way — the only possible way was the socialist way. Surely this is just the same kind of language?*

S. Yes, of course it is. Social psychologists have shown that that often happens on conversion. It doesn't have to be relativized. But the real question is this: does the whole of Christianity — the recognition and experience of Jesus as the Messiah — have to be interpreted simply as a social psychological phenomenon or is there something more in it? In other words, did God simply give his approval to ideals or visions or does he approve of people who have those ideals? Is he a God of ideals or is he a God of people? I think that, in the resurrection, God approves of a man — the person Jesus. He gives his definitive approval to the person Jesus and not just to his ideal.

O. *Does the story of Jesus' resurrection not belong to the same kind of language as the story of Elijah's ascension into heaven?*

S. Yes, both stories use the same kind of language. All the same, in the description of the resurrection and the various appearances and so on, existing models are used. That means, in other words, that there are experiences in human history that are expressed in that kind of model.

O. *But those 'experiences' were present even before the time of Jesus. The same linguistic data and images can be found in the Tenah, in the Old Testament . . .*

S. Yes, it is all there. Yet Jesus continues to be the great surprise.

O. *What, then, is the fundamental difference between Moses, Elijah and Jesus?*

S. The fact that there are similar models tells us nothing about the men to whom they are applied. The one is not a consequence of the other. Piet Schoonenberg was always very conscious of that. Are we the ones who project our images, expectations and visions on to Jesus or is it the historical figure of Jesus who, in the light of God's intention, projects something on to us? But it may also be the case — and this can be said not only on the basis of the figure of Jesus, but also on the basis of the whole ascending movement from the Old Testament up to Jesus and to everything that has developed from him — that God's definitive position is revealed here: people, that is how it has to be: he is the one, the definitive eschatological revelation. In other words, Jesus is God's unequivocal 'Yes' to men, the 'Yes' that cannot be reversed. In saying 'Yes' to us in this way, God hands himself over to us in Jesus and that gift is salvation for us and our salvation. The Bible calls this the 'kingdom of God'.

O. *What you are saying, then, is that the believing community wanted to say, in* *the story of Jesus and especially in the story of his resurrection that, at that particular moment in history, a word of God about the figure of Jesus of Nazareth sounded that had not sounded about Moses and Elijah, with whom he spoke on the mountain about his exodus?*

Jesus is certainly placed in the same context as Moses and Elijah in the gospel, but he is also raised up out of that context. Moses died and his eyes were closed by God. Elijah was taken up into heaven. Those are images that are closely related to the images used to evoke the resurrection. But what you are saying is that the Jesus community wanted to say more than this. Those early believers wanted to express their experience of the fact that, in Jesus of Nazareth, a more definitive, complete and lasting word of God had sounded. Is that correct?

S. Yes, that is what I have tried to say. The event can, of course, be interpreted exclusively or discriminatingly with regard to other religions or with regard to Moses and the other Old Testament prophets, but that would be a wrong interpretation. I would rather put it this way: what was made clear in Jesus is that God himself is salvation, universal salvation, for all people. That was made clear in him. It is, in other words, a question of the universal nature of the salvation that God prepares for all people without discriminating in any way between anyone.

O. *May we go back a little? Is it true to say that you believe, on the basis of the Judaeo-Christian tradition, that Jesus radicalized the Jewish 'law', the Torah, in word and deed in an unparalleled way?*

S. Yes, he radicalized the Torah and did so on his own authority. And that is something that I have not been able to find anywhere in the Old Testament. The prophets say: 'Thus says the Lord Yahweh', but Jesus says: 'I say to you'. Whether he said that literally or not, the fact is that he behaved in that way. For example, when he is speaking about marriage, he says: 'Moses says . . ., but I say . . .' and then he goes back beyond Moses to the original intention of God's creation. That is highly characteristic of Jesus. That is what he was like. I think that way of speaking on his own authority — and it occurs in all four gospels — was authentically Jesus. It also surprised those who heard him. It was not a Jewish way of speaking or rather, it was transcendent within Judaism. It went beyond the frontiers of Judaism. The prophets never speak in their own name. Radical statements were made, but they were always made on God's authority. Jesus, on the other hand, accepted the authority of the Torah, but spoke in his own name.

On the basis of all these converging data, I can accept the witness borne by the Judaeo-Christian tradition, in which Jesus is credited with a unique character — in whatever way that transcendent uniqueness is expressed — as a confession of faith. Something quite new, something that was not present in the tradition that preceded him, appeared in Jesus. And his death set the seal on that radically new element. He is called the 'Son of God' in the New Testament. That is one possible way of expressing this uniqueness. It is not the only way, but it is certainly one quite legitimate way.

O. *You have mentioned the story of the rich young man. You said Jesus radicalizes the Torah in it: 'Sell all that you have . . .' Do you see that radicalization as a way — for yourself, for modern man? Is it possible to 'sell everything', to 'distribute all that you have to the poor'? That young man in the story did not sell everything. You could almost say it is not feasible. That new way of life and everything that results from it in society — that complete revolution in the possession of money and property and in all human relationships — it simply hasn't happened! The Jesus movement does not consist of people who have 'sold everything'.*

S. That problem is also present in Luke's gospel. He was writing for a second and third generation of Christians, a very particular community, probably situated in a great city somewhere in the Roman Empire, outside Palestine. Obviously it was a middle-class community and its members certainly didn't sell everything. There were all kinds of conflicts between the rich and the poor! Luke wrote his gospel with those conflicts in mind. The scene that he sets is Jesus going into the hill district, praying throughout the night and then choosing twelve men from among his followers. Luke tells us that these men left everything for the sake of the kingdom of God. What the rich young man couldn't do, then, these twelve men were able to do.

Luke then says that Jesus came down from the mountain with the twelve to the 'great crowd of people' assembled there to touch him and be healed of their diseases by him. Then, according to Luke, Jesus presents those twelve men who had voluntarily accepted poverty to the assembled people — the 'great crowd' who, in Luke's gospel, consisted, you might say, of Luke's own middle-class Church. Those twelve poor followers, those men who have left everything for the kingdom of God, are, as it were, offered to the Church as an example. Jesus calls them blessed. In Luke 6:20, we read that Jesus looked at those disciples and said: 'Blessed are you poor' — and those 'poor' are, of course, the twelve he has chosen — 'for yours is the kingdom of God'.

In another part of his gospel, Luke presents Zacchaeus, the tax collector, to his church as an example. That is in chapter 19 and Luke tells us the tax collector was a rich man who promised to give half of his property to the poor. So we have two examples — first the twelve who had voluntarily become poor and then Zacchaeus, who gave away half of his possessions. These are held up before the people who belonged to his own community as orientation figures. We sit here and talk about whether we should make over two or three per cent of our income to the poor. Luke, however, says: 'Give half of your goods to the poor'! He is saying something very radical here — and he is saying it to the middle-class Church, which is what we in fact are. None of us gives half of our goods to the poor! But that is what Luke is asking the Church to do.

O. *So, in Jesus' preaching, the kingdom of God is absolutely central and the gospel presents those who want to belong to that 'kingdom' with a rule of life, a view of life, that is quite radical. It is: you must give away half of what you possess.*

S. Yes, and that is in fact just as radical in its effects as 'selling everything', because one person within the community will not have any more than another person. In that way, the community of believers will be an example to the world. They must, after all, be the beginning of a new human society and they can be in this way.

O. *That kind of distribution of property — that kind of intervention into the existing economic structures — is that the kingdom of God? Does the kingdom of God coincide, then, with a fundamental renewal of human society?*

S. I wouldn't use the word 'coincide' in that context. The kingdom of God certainly implies a renewal of our society. Making human society sound and whole, making all the relationships within that society whole — that is the coming of the kingdom of God, certainly. It is in that way that God's rule will be installed in our world.

O. *So where that takes place, the kingdom of God will take place?*

S. It will be near at hand.

O. *But why 'near at hand'? Is it possible to think of more than that? Can we expect more than a society of 'justice and love'?*

S. 'Near' because the kingdom of God always transcends what we can do to make it a reality. That is precisely its radical aspect.

O. *Let me just put myself in the position of people who say this: You are simply applying an ordinary Marxist socio-economic model to the gospel and what you have produced is an all too easy identification of the kingdom of God with a renewal of the structures of society — human rights for the poor, freedom, equality among men, the brotherhood and sisterhood of all people on earth. Are those people right? Is that not what you are doing?*

S. I am not simply identifying the kingdom of God with those things. That is why I said quite explicitly: The kingdom of God will be near at hand.

O. *What is the difference between 'The kingdom of God is there' and 'The kingdom of God is near at hand'?*

S. We never quite make justice and love a reality. It will always have to go further — radically further.

O. *Justice even in the smallest details? Freedom even in the most subtle relationships?*

S. Yes, it is not possible for us to imagine yet how far it goes. Whatever the kingdom of God may be for the rest, it certainly also means this. I don't think the kingdom of God will ever be fully realized and I hope the kingdom of God — where man's affair and God's affair coincide with each other — will in fact always transcend human history. But, of course, if you begin by saying that, you can put an immediate end to any attempt to make the kingdom of God a reality within the structures of society. And that would be a very wrong view of the kingdom of God.

O. *So, if we have done everything we can — is there still something on the credit side?*

S. Yes, there is. There is God himself. He coincides with nothing. The dividing line between him and us is not his dividing line, but ours. Anything that we may achieve in the way of social justice and love is always transcended by God himself. With regard to what has already been achieved, he is always absolutely new. He is never exhausted, certainly never in the kingdom that he establishes among us. There is always openness. We have to leave God his freedom in being new with regard to us — just as he has to respect our freedom in what we may realize in the way of salvation in this world. I prefer to see God not as an unchangeable and unchanging God, but rather as eternal youth. How should that thought be expressed, do you think? It transcends all our concepts.

God is new each day. He is a constant source of new possibilities. This is true not only with regard to our history, but also with regard to the end of our history — the eschaton. He is always surprising us. Even, I think, when we die. He is our perspective of life beyond death.

Let me express this idea in a slightly different way. God is absolute freedom. And that means that, as long as human history has not been completed, as long as the totality of history has not yet been given, we cannot know God's being — there is always something more and so there is always openness. And even that totality of history does not coincide with God's activity. It only points to the absolute source of freedom.

It is true, of course, that no being is completely absorbed in his activity. So we are bound to say that God is always a mystery and that he only reveals himself in concealment. His heart is greater than the end-result of history. That is one reason why we can dare to hope for 'eternal life', a life in which 'something new' can really be experienced.

O. *Is that idea, that suspicion, that God is 'absolute freedom' and 'new each moment' and that he is, as you say, 'our perspective of life beyond death' expressed in the gospel accounts of Jesus' resurrection?*

S. The idea that God transcends everything is, I think, to be found in certain prophetic texts such as Second Isaiah, in other words, it is expressed within Judaism itself. Just as the idea of resurrection from the dead and life after death were also expressed in the last two hundred or so years in Judaism before Christ's coming. That was not a new idea, first formulated by Christians. Jesus believed — it is quite clear from the gospel — in a God who transcended everything and he also believed in the resurrection from the dead.

The new and radical element in Jesus can be seen in his historical appearance. Wherever he went, the gospel tells us, communication was restored, people were healed, sins were forgiven and just relationships were established. What is the primary intention of the stories about Jesus' resurrection? Above all, they tell us that his life and message have a lasting value, that they remain valid. The confession of faith: 'He has risen' is first and foremost an interpretation of his life and message made by the first Christians, who are saying, in those resurrection stories: what Jesus did has a definitive, an absolute value and, if people do what he did, that too has a definitive, an absolute value. The primary significance of Jesus' resurrection is that God validates that way of life.

O. *Many people believe that the story of Jesus' resurrection is telling them that God is holding on to a man through death. When that passage from the gospel is read in the classical liturgy of the funeral service, that text in which Jesus says: 'I am the resurrection and the life; he who believes in me, though he die, yet shall he live' (Jn 11:25), what is being expressed, it seems to me, is faith and hope that God will bring that dead man or woman through death, just as he saved Jesus through death. What is evoked in the story of Jesus' resurrection is the hope that there is a life after death.*

S. The confession that 'Jesus has risen' also means, in the second place, I would say, that he was, in the whole of his life and even in his death, indissolubly linked to God, that his existential community with God was not destroyed by death. In other words, that living community continued through and beyond death in a very personal way and the same also applies to all those who have lived in the spirit of Jesus and have followed him. And following him means giving water to drink to the least of his brothers and sisters, the lowliest of people.

The account of Jesus' resurrection also has a third meaning. He rose and was exalted to God's right hand and in that state he continues to live in the community of his followers. He is present in the Church, pneumatically, breathing and inspiring. He is present wherever two or three are gathered together in his name, in other words, wherever people do what he did. That meaning is expressed in the New Testament in such phrases as 'He is the Lord' or 'the Lord is Spirit'.

O. *He is dead — but he lives? He disappeared from history, like everyone who dies — but he is active in history and in a unique way?*

S. According to human history, he is dead, yes, and we should not try to make light of this. He no longer exists. He is not there anymore. He is outside history. And yet, according to the resurrection stories, he lives with God and he is, what is more, the breath, the dynamism of the Christian community. And this is only meaningful if it means this: that God validates his existential praxis and that the way in which he lived and died, in the service of the poor and oppressed, has an absolute and definitive value in our history.

O. *The death of Martin Luther King or the death of Koos Koster — do they have the same definitive value?*

S. I would say . . . Yes, they do, in the light of a Christian interpretation. Martin Luther King consciously and explicitly chose to live as Jesus lived — his existential praxis. And he gave his life for that praxis. That is quite clear. In El Salvador, for example, a communist guerilla may not have any direct connection with Christianity, but, if he lays down his life for the liberation of his fellow-men, there is no essential difference. According to what is said in Mt 25, you are in the end judged by what you have done for the least of the brethren. You are not judged by how you justify your actions in the religious or ethical sense.

If you read that chapter in Matthew about the eschatological judgement, you can really get hold of what Jesus was about. In the end, we are judged by whether we have given water to the thirsty or whether we have helped the poor. In one sense, a purely atheistic judgment! But it expresses the very essence of Jesus' message. That whole passage sounds quite horizontal, even atheistic — what have you done for the poor? That is the appeal that is made to you. Then, at the end of the text, we have the interpretation: what you have done to your fellow-man, you have done to me. The poor man is identified with Jesus himself. To such an extent that the poor man who has received a glass of water is the one who judges, not Jesus. The poor man judges the extent to which we have demonstrated solidarity with him. In Jesus, God identifies himself with the poor man.

O. *So you would say radical commitment to one's fellow-man, going as far as dying for him, is doing what Jesus did. And that is validated by God?*

S. Yes. Man's affair is God's affiar. Well, if you commit yourself entirely to man's affair, whether you are Martin Luther King or a communist guerilla in El Salvador, you are in fact identifying yourself with God's affair, whether you are conscious of it or not.

O. *You said: The poor man judges the extent to which we have shown solidarity with him and that is God's judgement.*

S. Yes, that is so. The gospel identifies the poor man with the Son of Man, who identifies himself with God's affair. That is why the goats receive such a harsh sentence: 'Depart from me, you cursed!' If, on the other hand, you have shown solidarity with the poor, you will be invited in. According to Mt 25, it is the poor man who says: 'Come in'.

O. *If you translate this into political terms, you have the poor, exploited Third World countries' judgement of the United States and the rich West European countries. Do we, then, have to think of this as an eschatological judgement?*

S. That is what we are bound to conclude from an analysis of Mt 25. All that Matthew was doing was projecting the situation of his own times eschatologically.

O. *The judgement of those poor countries clearly includes a judgement of our socio-economic system in the West. What they are saying is: the structure of our society must be changed. Is that, in your opinion, what the gospel requires of us?*

S. Obviously the evangelists did not express it in precisely those terms. Their texts were historically conditioned. But if you read those texts in our present situation, with the possibility of structural change in mind — the change that must be brought about in North America and Western Europe — then that is certainly the only logical consequence.

O. *We heard of the murder of the four IKON journalists on 17 March 1982 and in the demonstration that followed you could see five crosses being carried. The demonstrators were going to plant them in the ground in front of the American Embassy. The biggest cross in the middle had the words: '40,000 Salvadorians'. The names of the four journalists were on the other four crosses. They had been quite spontaneously identified, in a people's liturgy, with the crucified Jesus. Anyone whose theology led him to believe that we have been 'once and for all time' redeemed and saved by the death of Jesus Christ alone would turn away in revulsion from that. But in your view it is obviously right that those names should appear on those crosses.*

S. Yes, it is right. You are very wide of the mark if you interpret the unique character of Jesus exclusively. That interpretation has often been made in the history of Christianity, in an attempt to avoid discovering Jesus in Buddhism, Islam and even in Israel. It is not in the spirit of Jesus himself, though. He did not proclaim himself, after all — he proclaimed God, the kingdom of God. He made it clear that man's affair was God's affair and he laid down his life for it and it was validated by God. So, wherever that happens, it is validated by God.

O. *So when it is said that Jesus is the Messiah, that is 'inclusive'. In other words, he is the messiah together with Martin Luther King and all those others, whether they know him or not and whether they recognize man's affair as God's affair or not?*

S. Yes. On the other hand, however, I would also say this: I would not know that without him. If he had not preceded us.

H. *You only know that it is inclusive through Jesus and you need him in order to hold on to this insight?*

S. It has been revealed to me in Jesus and made possible for us in him. It's not just a question of 'insight'. It is in him that my hope that it is also really possible and not just a vague utopia is based. Outside of him I cannot find really firm ground for that hope. Utopian expectations are historically quite effective, but they are very easily destroyed by critical reasoning.

Jesus just did it and even the most critical reasoning (that is not intent on its own advantage) cannot, in my opinion at least, produce any really plausible counter-arguments. My fundamental option is this: 'reason' itself has dimensions that transcend reason. My entire human option — what I have always opted for in my life — stands or falls by this. That is why I have always striven to be reasonable in my faith and faithful in my reasoning. That is for me the essential core of my whole life. I would even venture to say that this attitude to life — it would not be wrong to call it Thomistic — is why I am so opposed now to positivistic rationalism (of the kind that is predominant in so many of our universities) and to the (neo-) fundamentalism that attacks the very roots of our humanity under the guise of piety.

3

The power that came forth from him

O. *In the sixth chapter of Luke's gospel — you referred to this text earlier on, when you were describing the scene when Jesus, surrounded by his twelve disciples, came down from the hills and encountered a great crowd of people — there is a very suggestive sentence: a 'power came forth from him and healed them all'. This must mean, surely, that a spiritual power, a power of the spirit, came out of Jesus, touching and consoling people.*

Many members of the Christian 'community of faith' are more at home with these words about Jesus than they are with his 'miracles' — the healing of the man born blind, the raising of dead people or his changing water into wine and walking over the water. . . .

S. The miracles you have just mentioned are not historical events, so you can explain them fairly easily, that is, as the literary form of the proclamation of Jesus' unique appearance.

O. *Are all those other miracles historical events? Did they really happen?*

S. I would take as my point of departure the fact that there were many miracle-workers at that time, faith-healers and so on, of the kind that we still have today — people who possess certain powers, powers that are often called 'paranormal' nowadays. Many Jewish rabbis were 'miracle-workers' and, when Jesus was alive, there was even a special class of miracle-workers. For the people living at that time, then, there was no problem. Even those who were strongly opposed to Jesus had no difficulty with his 'miracles'. Their only real question was: From what source does his power come? Does he work those miracles in God's name or on the authority of Beelzebub — Satan, in other words? What is at work here in this man — the 'power of evil' or the 'power of God'?

We modern men are also confronted with a similar question: What really happened, historically? We cannot run away from that question.

I am personally convinced of the historical nature of two miracles. The first is the casting out of a devil, as reported in Lk 11:14–23: 'He was casting out a demon that was dumb'. The second is the healing of the centurion's servant (in, for example, Lk 7:1–10). These two facts are mentioned in all the traditions, even the so-called Q source, which preserves the oldest tradition, and so I regard them as authentic historical acts performed by Jesus. They are also the only miracles mentioned in Q and in each case the reference is very sober.

In the story of the casting out of a devil, the theme is not really the miracle itself, but the unknown authoritative element in Jesus' appearance. And that is interpreted as the presence of the kingdom of God — Jesus casts out devils with the 'finger of God' and he is also the eschatological prophet. That is what this particular miracle story is concerned with.

In the story of the cure of the centurion's servant, the real theme is once again not so much the healing miracle as the faith of that man, the Roman officer. Jesus says: 'Not even in Israel have I found such faith' and, when the man goes home, he finds his servant healed. Well, whatever may have happened and whatever the precise details of the event may be, that does not really concern me. What does concern me is this: in that context, that particular healing was for that man a miracle.

Just imagine — my father is very ill and the doctors hold out no hope for him. I pray to God for his recovery and he is in fact cured. May I not regard that as an answer to my prayer, God's answer, even though I know the doctor has cured him or there has been some 'good luck'? If I really take as my point of departure my own relationship with God, a relationship in which I speak to him in prayer, asking him to make my father well again, that is for me a miracle, a sign from God.

So there are two historical miracles in the New Testament. All the others — the raising of the widow of Nain's son and so on — are later additions to the original story, literary forms based on Old Testament texts: when the ultimate prophet, the Messiah, has come, he will perform these and other miracles, the miracles listed in Second Isaiah, for example, the blind will see, the lame will leap, the lepers will be cleansed and so on. From the moment people were convinced that this man Jesus was really the eschatological prophet, he had in fact done what had been described in Second Isaiah and his miracles were expressed as a theme. The miracles are in fact composed as a theme.

O. *So what you are saying is that there was a moment in history when Jesus was recognized as the ultimate prophet and Messiah. Miracles were attributed to him although he had never in fact performed them as historical events. This was the way in which the healing and liberating power that came forth from him was described, following the tradition and in accordance with the vision of Second Isaiah. The miracle stories, in other words, are the literary form in which the testimony: 'He is the Messiah' is expressed. Have I summarized your ideas correctly?*

S. Yes, you have. On the basis of the whole of Jesus' life and of two historical and extremely striking facts.

O. *But what do you mean by 'historical' facts here? What you said is: these two facts appear in all the sources and so they are historical.*

S. And so they are historical. That's my conclusion, but, from the purely historical point of view, of course, it is no more than a hypothesis.

O. *It strikes me as a bit dubious to speak in that case of 'two historical miracles'. If I am not mistaken, you postulated the historicity of those miracles in your* Jesus, an Experiment in Christology *in order to prevent the testimony 'He is the Messiah' from being simply beating the air, giving rise to a kind of ideology about Jesus that is unrelated to the historical Jesus who set people, historical people, free at that time and in that place from the 'power of evil'.*

Could we not say, for instance: It is historically certain that such a great and unique power came from him that the same examples were used again and again in the earliest testimonies about him in order to demonstrate that power?

S. Yes, that is how it ought to be expressed.

O. *To say that is to say a great deal! The 'historical' element that we know with certainty is therefore that there was a power in Jesus which changed men's lives. And that was a new beginning in Israel.*

S. He was the beginning of a movement that was to reach to the farthest corners of the earth. That was also how he saw himself — as a beginning. It is quite clear that he was not concerned with himself. He was above all concerned with the kingdom of God that had to have its roots in men and women. In the whole of his preaching, Jesus is like the mustard-seed that has great power in itself.

O. *In one of his sayings, he says that his followers were going to work greater miracles than he did.*

S. I don't know whether that is one of Jesus' own words or not, but it doesn't matter very much. What emerges from the whole of the New Testament is that the Christian community is conscious of the need to continue Jesus' work and to liberate people from injustice and oppression.

H. *Surely a liberation involving the whole of nature and not just people — a liberation humanizing nature, as Marx put it?*

S. Yes, nature as well as man. What is man, after all? He lives in an environment — an ecological environment. Man must become quite sound together with the whole of his ecological environment. There is a whole ecological theology in America.

O. *If man is really liberated so that he can be fully human, he will have a different relationship with the earth, with animals and plants and with water and air. Pablo Neruda has said:*

> *'Then the day will come*
> *when we will liberate*
> *light and water,*
> *earth and man.*
> *Then it will be:*
> *all things for all men'.*

These words are sung as part of the liturgy in some critical communities of Christians.

S. Salvation has to be made a reality in every human dimension on earth. That is what the biblical image of 'a new heaven and a new earth' points to and that is the perspective of liberation.

O. *The real miracle, I think, is the emergence and continued existence of the movement that we call Christianity throughout the history of man up to the present day. The one from whom such great power came is the miracle and the community of believers who work to make justice and love a living reality — that community is the 'even greater' miracle. Would you agree that this is the essential message expressed in the miracle stories?*

S. Yes, I would. It is the miracle of Pentecost — a miracle that occurs again and again at the best moments in the whole history of the Messianic movement. It is from this miracle that we derive a power . . . a power we can only experience as grace, but a power that is not in any way alien or unknown to us.

O. *I would like to quote one or two things Rob Sijmons wrote about you on 25 July 1981 in the newspaper* Vrij Nederland. *You may remember his article: 'The Controversial* Quod Erat Demonstrandum *of the theologian and historian Schillebeeckx'. Sijmons says: 'To defend his historical analysis of Jesus, Schillebeeckx resorts to the "constant factor" of the "Christian movement itself", people who have, throughout the centuries, found "fundamental salvation from God in Jesus of Nazareth" and a "Christian unity of experience" '. Then he inserts a little phrase: 'Halleluiah ought to be sufficient commentary' and goes on to say: 'Well, it would seem that there is a prophet who preaches the gospel of unidentified flying objects. After a thorough study of his concrete examples of "appearances", little or nothing is left intact of all the available data. We can, however, evaluate the true nature of flying saucers and similar objects by means of the "constant factor". Despite all the evidence to the contrary, there is still a movement of people, the UFO movement, who believe in flying saucers.' And Rob Sijmons concludes this part of his article with the words: 'What a science!'*

Would you say this was fallacious thinking on Sijmon's part or is your argument a bit faulty here and there?

S. A comparison of that kind, in which the author speaks of the 'gospel of unidentified flying objects', points clearly to the positivism and objectivism of so much scientific thinking these days. It is very widespread both among believers and among non-believers. Sijmon's thinking is wrong because his presuppositions are positivistic. The 'gospel of unidentified flying objects' has nothing to do with the person who might proclaim a 'gospel' of that kind. The gospel of justice, on the other hand, has everything to do with the one who proclaims it. It is not in any sense legitimate to objectivize Jesus' proclamation of the gospel of justice and to speak scientifically of flying saucers that can be empirically verified or proved false. The gospel of justice is indissolubly linked to the person who proclaims it and at the same time also to the praxis of the contemporary Christian movement. The only valid approach to this question is hermeneutic, not scientific, in the sense of natural science. It rather looks as though Sijmons still adheres to the outdated nineteenth-century view that the natural sciences constitute the model for all other scientific approaches, including that of theology. What a theory of science!

4

'He who has seen me has seen the Father'

O. *The Our Father is one of the central texts in which the unique figure of Jesus is recognized and experienced within the community of believers. It has become the central prayer, both personally and in the liturgy.*

S. Jesus' message is fully expressed in the Our Father, yes. There are, of course, two versions, one in Matthew and the other in Luke. The Lucan version is shorter and, in all probability, it is the oldest form. It is, after all, hardly likely that a prayer used by Jesus himself and then used by members of the Christian community in their gatherings would, with the passage of time, have been shortened. It would undoubtedly have been made longer. So the shorter version is probably the earlier one.

The Our Father is a prayer with a strong eschatological orientation: 'Thy kingdom come', 'Hallowed be thy name'. Those are eschatological prayer formulae. They are prayers that look forward to the great end, the end of time, the fulfilment. Even the prayer for bread is eschatological — Matthew has: 'Give us this day our bread for tomorrow'. It is the bread of life, life itself. But that great day has to begin now, today: 'Give us this day'. And the kingdom of God breaks through now. It is already here and it is manifested in the fact that others forgive us our guilt and sin and that we forgive others. That reconciliation between people — it is in that that the kingdom of God breaks through and it breaks through now. And in that mutual reconciliation God's name is made holy, here and now. And then we have: 'And lead us not into temptation'. That is, of course, the great temptation that will take place at the end of time. We pray that we shall not cease to believe then.

O. *What is that temptation? How should we think of it — God 'leading us into temptation'?*

S. That prayer can be traced back to the Jewish evening prayer. It is stated in a number of rabbinical commentaries: God does not lead us into temptation. The temptation is already present, persecution for the sake of faith, being put to the test in a world in which the right of the strongest prevails. In the Our Father, we pray that we shall be able to endure in being put to the test. What we are asking is: Let us stand firm when it comes to the pinch. Let us hold our ground in those extreme situations, when it seems as though we have been cut off from the future.

O. *The beginning of the prayer — Jesus says 'Father'.*

S. In Luke it begins with 'Father'. In Matthew, Jesus says 'Our Father'.

O. *It is in that intimate way of speaking to God, so we are told, that the Old Testament differs from the New and that the specific sonship of Jesus is expressed. But we only have to reflect for a moment about that and we are at once confronted with great difficulties, because that unique sonship of Jesus puts him at a distance from us — God is his father in a way that is different from the way in which he is our father or else he is more his father than ours. What is the real significance of that address: 'Our Father'?*

S. I think the Christian community had trouble with it to begin with. The Jewish Christians must have found it especially difficult to call God 'Abba'. It is clear from the rabbinical literature that the word 'Abba', which had the emotive force of our 'Dad' or 'Daddy', was not used in the liturgy. But Jesus obviously wanted his disciples to pray 'Abba' in that prayer. In the gospel of John, the words 'my Father and your Father' are placed on Jesus' lips. Many theologians have concluded from this that he wanted to make a clear distinction here between his own sonship, his relationship with the Father, and the relationship between Christians and the Father. But, within the context of the whole of the gospel of John, it is quite clear that he means: my Father who has now also become your Father.

O. *Has become?*

S. Yes, has *become* our Father, through the preaching of Jesus and through his whole appearance. Those who listened to that preaching and were 'converted' to the kingdom of God — he became *their* Father.

O. *What you are saying is: listening to Jesus' preaching makes the listeners sons and daughters, children of the Father and enables them to enter into that relationship that Jesus himself had with his Father. They are, in other words, 'born of God'.*

S. Yes. But you can't draw any direct conclusions from that exceptional use of 'Abba' about what is generally known as Jesus' unique sonship. The very opposite is true: Jesus wanted to show that those who followed him would have exactly the same relationship with God as Father.

O. *But in the dogmatic theology of the Church, Jesus of Nazareth is still called the unique son of God. He is simply called the Son — that recurrent formula: 'In the name of the Father and of the Son and of the Holy Spirit' — the pre-existent Son and even 'Jesus is God'. Catholics are taught that and it occurs again and again in the liturgy.*

S. What I am saying is that that conclusion cannot be directly drawn from the unique use of the word 'Abba' by Jesus in the New Testament. Oh, the New Testament certainly makes it quite clear that Jesus' mission was based on an intimate relationship with God — his mission was like that of Moses, who associated with God as one friend with another. In the later New Testament texts, there is clear evidence of growing veneration of Jesus — you cannot help noticing the increase in the number of titles of sovereign majesty and there are even a few texts in which it is more or less said: 'He is God'. But that is not the general tendency. It cannot be found even in Paul, who sees Jesus above all as subordinate to the Father, to God.

In John's gospel, where Jesus is presented as the great, pneumatic Lord who has come from heaven to us, there are the words: 'The Father is greater than I'. Several theologians have interpreted this as meaning that Jesus was speaking then 'according to his humanity' and not 'according to his divinity'. But none of that is, of course, to be found in the gospel of John, in which Jesus is seen simply as a man, although he *is*, I admit, seen as a man who had a unique relationship with God and whose nature was — and I would say this very emphatically — so mysterious that we cannot define it theoretically. It is quite understandable, within the context of fourth and fifth-century thought, that an attempt to define that mysterious nature of Jesus theoretically was made at Chalcedon. All the same, it is very dangerous to make such attempts. To attempt to define Jesus' nature is to limit it, to narrow it down, to bring it to a point that may well be too sharp, with the result that Jesus is either underestimated or overestimated.

O. *Do you think they overestimated Jesus at Chalcedon?*

S. The statement that Jesus is *the* unique Son of God — *that* dogma, *that* profession of faith does what other formulae in the tradition of our faith have done: it gives direction to our faith. But it is at the same time a profession of faith formulated within a clearly defined Middle Platonic philosophical framework.

O. *It is a profession of faith — you have to think of those words as a hymnic or liturgical formula rather than as a dogmatic one, I feel.*

S. Yes, I would agree with you without hesitation, because every good dogmatic definition is always doxological. It is always an expression of praise and honour, said or sung during liturgical celebration. It can be prepared in theological discussion, yes, but the declaration of dogma itself is a doxology.

O. *It's a hymn, then?*

S. It's a hymn. You have to interpret those words hymnically. But they have, of course, been taken from the philosophical language of that period and so they can't be detached from that fabric. If you try to unpick the stitching and proclaim the words as truth in themselves — Chalcedon says Jesus is 'truly God and truly man' — and if you separate that confession of faith from the question to which an answer was sought at that time, well, then everything will turn out wrongly.

O. *What was that question to which an answer was sought then?*

S. The question was whether God's salvation had in fact been definitively given in the man Jesus. Arius and the theologians who were thought to be teaching heresy during the early centuries of Christianity failed not so much because they had a wrong view of Jesus' relationship with God as because they did not postulate Jesus definitively as God's salvation for all men. The reaction of the Church at that time was: salvation has been given once and for all time in Jesus. And that claim was justified theoretically by saying: then he must have been God himself, appearing in humanity, because definitive salvation can only be God himself. It was really an attempt to safeguard that faith in definitive, eschatological salvation in Jesus.

O. *As the Son of God, Jesus is 'one in being with the Father' — what is your view of this?*

S. That was what was said at the First Council of Nicaea in 325 A.D. That was, of course, an attempt to express the extent of the intimacy between Jesus and the Father. The word 'consubstantial' was used for 'one in being', but we can't grasp the meaning of that concept now, whether we say 'consubstantial', 'one in being' or 'one in substance' with the Father. That's not just because it is such a learned term, but . . . what is being 'one in substance' with God? It is obvious from the New Testament that Jesus is one with God in will and action. We have, for example, the saying: 'Not as I will, but as thou wilt' (Mt 26:39), when Jesus was praying to the Father in the garden. It is possible to think here of a mystical communion with God, but that is restricting. A Hellenistic view was used in the Church's dogma and God and Jesus were declared to be one in being.

O. *That Hellenistic view is expressed on Sundays in most Roman Catholic churches in the creed. Quite often it is sung. The language is hymnic. But how do you explain that term: 'one in being'? I am assuming these words should not be left out.*

S. No, we should keep them in the creed.

O. *I agree, because they have been handed down to us in a very long tradition. But how can they be explained to us now?*

S. That is in theory very difficult to do. In practice, there is no problem. Some Christians would like to see the creed renewed and various attempts have been made to do so. I think it is quite right to formulate modern creeds — if we Christians have any real self-respect, we are bound in the long run to do that. At the same time, however, I think the old creed ought to be retained for all Christians, as a standard liturgical hymn, a kind of shared sign of recognition. It shouldn't be touched. It has, I know, become unintelligible, at least parts of it have, but it has a function in the liturgy as a sign of recognition. But it certainly requires explanation. The Our Father also gives rise to a greater number of questions, but that doesn't mean the text ought to be changed.

O. *'One in being' is obviously not a biblical way of speaking. But you said it should be understood as Jesus' being one attitude or one in will and vision with the Father. Or is that perhaps not saying enough?*

S. I would like to add a little to that. Jesus identifies himself in his vision, his message and also in his death completely with God himself and God identifies himself with that man Jesus — that is clear from the resurrection. There is, then, a personal, prophetic identification. As a theologian, however, I would prefer not to use the term 'one in being' any more, because of its special and historically conditioned background.

O. *I find that very strange. You say: as a theologian I would prefer not to use it, but yet you think it ought to be retained in the liturgy?*

S. I admit that seems to be a difficult point. But don't forget the liturgy is expressed in metaphorical language.

O. *Liturgical language surely becomes empty and alien if it can no longer be explained and interpreted! So we've got to find ways of doing it!*

S. That is true, certainly. But the early formulae don't have to be disputed. They express the Christian message adequately in a way that was characteristic and decisive at the time when they were made. They act as a kind of signpost for us now, pointing in the direction we should follow in search of other key-words. The way of saying something is not what is really said. We have to preserve what is really said, but we can and must change the way of saying it.

It is possible to say: in being he is one with the Father. Our modern phrase 'in being' has nothing at all to do with the Greek word *ousia*, nor has our phrase 'in substance' any connection with the Latin *substantia*. So in being, if that really matters, he is one with the Father.

O. *Jesus, then, is 'in being one with the Father'* — *in the ultimate, eschatological sense, do you mean?*

S. Yes, but in a manner that this eschatological element in Jesus is already a reality here and now. I would put it this way: In Jesus' personal history, that is, in the 'history of his being', in other words, in the way that he followed in his life, death and resurrection — it is in this way that Jesus' being was expressed — the being of God the Father is united and revealed in one single event, disclosed to us and, what is more, disclosed as salvation for all people.

You can only really grasp the distinctive nature of the man Jesus if you think of him as being the definitive centre of the revelation of the being of God himself. God's being is love of men and Jesus' life is just as much love of men, in identification with his Father. You have to look at the man

Jesus to know who God is. 'He who has seen me has seen the Father' — these words are in the gospel of John (Jn 14:9). It is possible therefore to understand what 'one in being' means nowadays without appealing to Greek philosophy.

O. *Let us go back a little way. I remember we said all those who follow Jesus are sons and daughters, children, people of God. Are they also children of God 'in being'? Are people who commit themselves to the kingdom of God, to justice and peace, one in being with the Father, with God, as Jesus was?*

S. I would say they are really one in being with him, but thanks to Jesus.

O. *What do you mean: thanks to Jesus?*

S. In relation to Jesus. Insofar as they follow Jesus, they share in his life. The unique character of Jesus is to be found in his preceding us, going ahead of us.

O. *And do you have to know him and give your consent to him as the one who 'goes ahead' in order to be 'his follower'? I think there are many people who 'follow' him. I mean, who do what he did, even though they do not know him or give their consent to him explicitly.*

S. I admit that's quite possible.

O. *And doing justice — does that also make you one in being with the Father?*

S. Yes, it does. Once more, I would point in this case too to Matthew 25 — if you give a glass of water to the least of men, then you are one of those to whom it is said: 'Come, O blessed of my Father'. But that doesn't mean we can do it just as well without Jesus.

O. *Why doesn't it?*

S. Knowledge of God's grace, his gift to us, is in itself a grace and we are at once required to honour, praise and thank God. If we don't have that knowledge and still follow the way on which Jesus has gone ahead of us, there is something missing. You don't *know* . . . well, how should I put it? There is a shortcoming.

O. *And that shortcoming is present in Judaism, for example. Would you say that? In following the Torah and doing God's will and living according to his vision in that way, the Jews suffer from a shortcoming? In comparison with those who do the same, but in the name of Jesus?*

S. It's never a question of a subjective shortcoming as such. Jews may well be an example for Christians, a reproach to them, by living in justice and working for it. Jesus, after all, said of an 'unbeliever', in this case a non-Jew: 'Not even in Israel have I found such faith'. And it is that faith that is so important. That's why 'objective' comparisons are so often misleading.

On the other hand, the Christian should not give up the deepest conviction of his life. He cannot cease to believe that the definitive revelation of salvation from God, a revelation that is absolutely central, but not exclusive, is intimately connected with Jesus as the unique one of Israel.

The difference can never be traced exclusively to a difference between knowing and not knowing. It is situated at a much deeper level. What is at stake here is the fullness of God's saving activity in history. And that does not necessarily mean that Christians are always the most faithful and effective in giving their consent to that fullness of God's work of salvation and in making it a reality in the world.

5

Jesus, the unique one of Israel

O. *How do you see the relationship between Jesus and Israel?*

S. In the first place, we should not forget that Jesus was a Jew. He was a religious figure within Israel, not outside it. The first interpretations of Jesus were not 'Christian' — they were Jewish. All those key-concepts such as 'eschatological prophet', the 'Son of man', 'Son of God' and so on — they are all Jewish concepts. The first Christians were therefore regarded as 'schools' within Israel and as similar to the Pharisees, the Sadducees or the Essenes. No one thought, at least to begin with, that the Jews who followed Jesus were outside Judaism.

Even Paul says quite explicitly: salvation comes from the Jews. They were the olives on to which the others were grafted. God chose Israel and that situation was not changed when Jesus was chosen. Jesus' election is a concentration of the election of the entire Jewish people, just as, at an earlier period of history, the history of Israel, that election had been concentrated in the king of Israel and in the suffering servant to whom Second Isaiah refers in those songs.

God did not in any way regret his gifts. What was at stake was salvation for all men without exception, but through Israel. Salvation would have been no more than an abstraction if it had not been made a concrete reality in particular historical data and events, in a particular people. Later it was concentrated in the man Jesus.

H. *Paul may have insisted on the very close link between Christianity and Judaism, but it didn't last very long. In his book on Christian theology since*

Auschwitz, Hans Jansen says again and again that the New Testament itself is tainted with anti-Judaism.

S. It is certainly said that the Church is the true Israel in the New Testament, but, on the basis of Paul's teaching, we are bound to attack that idea. We are bound to say that this New Testament criticism of Israel is a mistaken form of theology, although we should not forget there was also a great deal of criticism of the Jews whose faith in Yahweh was concentrated exclusively on worship in the Temple and that criticism was expressed above all by the Hellenistic Jews of the diaspora.

The criticism of the Jews that is found in the New Testament is, of course, above all a criticism of Jews made by Jews — Jewish Christians. The most anti-Jewish document in the New Testament is the gospel of John and that can be traced back to a mystical Jewish movement in Palestine. That criticism in the New Testament is based on the model of prophetical criticism of the leaders of Israel and is not so much a criticism of Israel as such. Jesus himself says, in the synoptic gospels, that he has sympathy with the people, because they are without leaders, 'sheep without a shepherd'. If Hans Jansen intends to provide evidence of anti-Judaism in the New Testament in the sequel to his book *Christian Theology since Auschwitz*, then, in my opinion at least, he will be very wide of the mark.

H. *But what happened when the Church became increasingly a Church of gentiles, rather than a Church of Jews and gentiles?*

S. The gentile Christians began to accuse the Jews of not having accepted Jesus and there were mutual excommunications. Non-Christian Jews also condemned Christians for establishing an irregular school within Judaism. At quite an early stage, a curse against Christians was included in the Shemoneh Esreh, the prayer of the eighteen benedictions. And the Fathers of the Christian Church quite soon began to call Israel unfaithful. The rupture between Jew and gentile need never have happened just because Jesus was called the Messiah by Jewish Christians. It did not take place because of him. It came about as a result of historical circumstances. The drama, however serious it may have been, was historically contingent.

O. *What you are saying, then, is that Judaism and Christianity went their separate ways because of historical circumstances. But if you take the historical contingency of God's concentration of his election in Jesus as your point of* *departure, surely it is possible to say that the Jews' rejection of Jesus is not, in its historical contingency, of such critical importance?*

S. I think two different concepts of contingency play a part in this. The whole of Jesus' incarnation and his entire appearance in our history is, of course, a historical fact and is therefore situated in the contingency of our human history. Our attitude towards Jesus, whether we are for or against him, is in the same way historically contingent. But our attitude also contains a new element — an element of choice: Are you for or against Jesus? Two different tendencies can quite easily be distinguished in the New Testament. The first is: Whoever is not for Jesus is against him. The second is: Whoever is not against Jesus is for him.

O. *What are you for, then, if you are for Jesus?*

S. That is very clear from his preaching: Seek first the kingdom of God and his righteousness. Wherever there is justice done by men and women, there is the kingdom of God. That is the most important reality of all. That 'being for Jesus' has all too often been transferred simply to the level of men's minds in the Catholic tradition, but that is altogether too idealistic. Righteousness — justice — has to be a reality.

H. *The so-called Old Testament has always played a very important part in the debate between Judaism and Christianity. Many Dutch theologians, members of the Reformed Churches, have drawn our attention to this fact. K. H. Miskotte, for example, said in his book,* Hoofdsom der historie: *'The Old Testament came first. Then we have the New Testament. Then, once again, we have the Old Testament, since a whole set of promises from the Old Testament have not yet been fulfilled'. What do you think about this credit that is found in the Old Testament?*

S. The Tenah or Old Testament is a book about Jews and Christians. The credit found in the Old Testament is a credit that is applied both to Jews and to Christians. In other words, there is a Jewish interpretation and a Christian interpretation of the Old Testament. Both interpretations are possible. We Christians have so often thought that the Old Testament was concluded with the New, that is, with Jesus. But that idea has no validity for the Jews.

There are, then, two legitimate interpretations — one made in the light of the new situation created by Jesus and the other the Jewish interpretation, which has its own special value and is not in any way terminated by the Christian interpretation of the Tenah. According to his own words,

Jesus did not come to abolish the law. It is no longer even a possibility to carry out a campaign to convert the Jews to faith in Christ. They can, in being Jews, possess precisely what Jesus himself proclaimed.

H. *I would like to quote from the correspondence between Franz Rosenzweig, who had remained a Jew, and his friend Eugen Rosenstock, a Jew who had become a Christian. They exchanged letters during the First World War and in one of them Rosenzweig wrote: 'All Jews are bound to find the Christian's relationship with God inadequate and circuitous. Surely it goes almost without saying that we should call God our Father — we do not need anyone, whoever it may be, to teach us to do that! There is no need for a third person between me and my Father in heaven!' What do you think of that statement?*

S. I think it is one view. In the letter to the Hebrews, however — and that has a very marked Jewish background — it is said quite clearly that we can only gain direct access to the Father through Jesus. In the case of the Jews, this took place through the high-priest, who entered the Holy of Holies once a year. With Jesus, on the other hand, we no longer need this kind of mediation. That's the tenor of the letter to the Hebrews, at least.

You can, however, also look at it from another point of view and say: Israel is God's son and also does not need a mediator. He can go personally and directly to the Father. But then there is the fact that the whole of the Tenah is one long accusation: Israel never responds to God's faithfulness.

H. *Is there also something on the credit side for Christians in the Old Testament?*

S. For Christians, the Bible is not just the New Testament — it is the New and the Old Testament. If you simply take the New Testament on its own, there is always a danger that you will come under the influence of Jesus to such a degree that the whole of his background, in other words, the Old Testament, pales into insignificance beside him.

H. *But did the New Testament authors not intend to make the Old Testament pale into insignificance beside him?*

S. No, I don't think so. That only came about in the course of history and fairly recently at that. It's widely believed that Christians have always lived from the New Testament, but that it is only since the thirteenth century that the New Testament began to play a much more important part for Christians than the Old. During the Middle Ages and the patristic period, the Church lived above all from the Old Testament. The evidence of this is to be found in the mosaics in very early churches and the stained glass windows of so many cathedrals. I remember very well a film I once saw about a church in Calabria in Italy. The whole of the Old Testament was depicted in that church and then, at the very end of the film there were three little scenes showing Jesus preaching, dying and rising again. It was only when the New Testament appeared in the language of the people and there was a great movement of evangelization in the twelfth and thirteenth centuries that the emphasis began to change.

O. *But even though this change of emphasis from the Old to the New Testament took place quite late in the history of Christianity, it was always assumed that everything in the Old Testament had been fulfilled in Jesus. This meant that an enormous claim was made by the Christian Church in its dialogue with Israel. After listing everything that Jesus did and fulfilled, you can say in four simple words: He is the fulfilment.*

S. Yes, but, on the other hand, there is a tendency nowadays to subject the whole of the New Testament to the criticism of the Old. And it is certainly true to say the whole of the New Testament can only be read in the light of the Old. The first Christians interpreted Jesus in the light of their knowledge of the Old Testament. So we are bound to say the Old Testament has a very special significance for Christians, as a counter-balance to an excessive concentration on Jesus. After all, Jesus did not place the emphasis on himself. He always stressed the kingdom of God. And the kingdom is pre-eminently a Jewish idea.

H. *So it is even possible to claim that, without the Old Testament, the New Testament pales into insignificance?*

S. Yes, I think so. Without the Old Testament, the New Testament is really an apocryphal book. Marcion wanted to do away with the Old Testament and he was quite rightly condemned for heresy.

H. *You may remember a recent discussion on the Dutch television programme* Between Cologne and Paris *in which Jews and Christians talked almost exclusively about one thing: what Christians could learn from Jews. Then, at one point in the programme, one of the rabbis who was present asked the question: what can Jews learn from Christians? No one could answer that question! Would you have been able to answer it if you had taken part in that programme?*

S. Since Auschwitz, this is a question that has seriously embarrassed Christians, so much so that they hardly dare to answer it. All the same, I think we ought to have the courage of 'converts', in other words, the courage of people who recognize their guilt with regard to Judaism, confess it openly and at the same time take care not to betray their own Christianity.

I believe that God's revelation, as expressed in the Jew Jesus, also includes the fact that Israel's history of suffering, which culminated in Jesus' life and death, is God's definitive revelation.

There is a definitive link between salvation from God and Jesus' manner of living and dying and therefore, because it is definitive, that link is also 'eschatological'. Messianic salvation cannot be simply left open at random. History is certainly always open, but salvation can never be obtained in a purely arbitrary fashion. Jesus, who was Israel's son, reveals God's power over history, but he does not do this in one or another form of rule or supremacy, such as kingship, priesthood or even abstract human ideals. He does it rather in the form of impotence — the impotence of one who was crucified.

God identified himself with someone who was crucified, someone who died as one who had been rejected by society and by the religious leaders of that society. That history is liberating. However open history may be, it must, from the Christian point of view, be a history of 'following Jesus'. Then it is a history of salvation.

Those who suffer and are rejected are both the object of revelation (it is their salvation that is involved) and the subject of revelation (they are the only ones who can speak with authority about revelation). God's last word about human history is not a word of condemnation or anger — it is a word of mercy and liberation. This provides the basis for lasting hope. On that hope, we can even now work for the improvement of our history. And we *must* work to improve that history!

There is no place in this for vague, utopian thoughts. The witness borne by martyrs of all kinds to justice is always a source of powerful historical impulses that lead to good. God's last word also provides the basis for a realistic attitude that is opposed to all naive faith that human beings will of their own accord become so wise that they will be able to bring about an authentic 'earthly paradise'.

If the Christian interpretation is right and universal salvation is concentrated in Jesus — concentration does not, remember, imply exclusivism! — then this really points to a relativization of many laws of the Torah, such as circumcision and so on. Paul was not the first person to think of this. It was already present, at least as a germinal idea, in the message of John the Baptist and that of Jesus himself. This relativization is also important when we think of the world religions. The concentration of salvation in Jesus is also a liberation of salvation from factors that restrict it and deprive it of its freedom . . .

H. *What possibilities are there, do you think, in the future for conversations between Jews and Christians?*

S. It is not so difficult to envisage dialogue at the theological level in the future. The biggest problem of all in this dialogue is undoubtedly Auschwitz.

O. *Auschwitz also in the sense of a milestone on a road that leads through the whole of human history?*

S. Yes, although I myself would not follow Hans Jansen, for example, all the way in the argument that he uses in his *Christian Theology since Auschwitz*. He has, I admit, done very well to pile up fact after fact for us, but I would have liked an analysis of the social and economic background to those facts. And I object to the way in which he links Auschwitz and the whole of Hitler's persecution of the Jews so closely to Christianity. That seems to me to be historically unjustified. When eleventh and twelfth-century Christians made Jews wear the Star of David they were doing something which had a different meaning from what was done by Hitler in this century. I also think Jansen does not emphasize sufficiently the fact that Christian anti-Semitism is a variant of the anti-Semitism that existed long before Christianity in the Middle East. Christians did not invent anti-Semitism, although they did, with their theology of the 'murder of God' impose a distinctively Christian impression on anti-Semitism.

It is a great pity Jansen's book is basically a summary of a number of texts and not a historical study. I could, for example, place alongside a list of accusations against the Jews a parallel list of accusations against such heretics as Marcion, Arius and so on (almost in the same words). Those accusations would consist of very much the same clichés and vituperations, but applied on the one hand to Jews and, on the other, to Marcionites, Nestorians and so on. What both sets of vituperations would amount to is this: everything that is not part of the universal Christian truth — 'Catholic' truth, you might say — is false teaching and belongs to the devil . . .

A historian would, of course, have the task of analysing this universal phenomenon. It is only after he has done this that he would be able to form a historically justified judgement about specifically Christian anti-Semitism. This, however, has so far not been done! If it had been done, then the radically new and specific aspect of modern anti-Semitism since the time of the nineteenth-century German philosophers would have been recognized for what it is. Jansen's book has very serious failings from the historical point of view and I am afraid the lesson the author wants to teach us will be knocked to pieces by historical criticism and that's a pity.

O. *What should our attitude as Christians be, do you think, towards the fact of Auschwitz and the whole history of Christian anti-Semitism?*

S. It would be impossible to delete the whole of that history — and a great deal has happened in it, of course, even just in the pronouncements that the Church has made against the Jews. I believe the Church ought to say, quite clearly, solemnly and officially, *mea culpa*. As long as that doesn't happen and as long as the pope does not make a clear declaration, it will continue to be the affair of a handful of pioneers and not the affair of the Church itself.

O. *So you are asking the Church and the whole of its hierarchy to confess its guilt. We can't forgive ourselves for Auschwitz — only the Jews themselves can forgive us. But forgiveness can only take place if guilt is confessed.*

S. Yes, *only* if guilt is confessed. That is very much a doctrine of the Church!

O. *Why doesn't it happen, then? John XXIII had that terrible text about the Jews taken out of the Good Friday liturgy and asked for forgiveness for the murder of the Jews in the form of a personal prayer. What has to be done before the Church will officially confess guilt?*

S. It hasn't happened so far because the Church is still involved in a kind of Christian anti-Semitism. There are all kinds of twists and turns even in the Decreee on the Jews composed during the Second Vatican Council, although that document is very open compared to what the Church had to say about the Jews before that time.

O. *But it is still an inadequate text, you think?*

S. Yes, it is quite inadequate. I can imagine great care was taken not to obscure the fact that Jesus was murdered by his fellow-men, because, after all, it was not God who killed his son, but men and, in the concrete, Romans and Jews. But you can see that Pilate and the Roman authorities are exonerated even in the New Testament — in Mark's gospel — because Christianity had, in the meanwhile, spread to include the Romans. The Jews, on the other hand, have to take more and more of the blame, although, from the historical point of view, the whole event was much more complicated than that. Jesus was crucified and that means that it was a Roman legal action.

O. *Can you indicate how the Church's confession of guilt could be made — how the wall dividing Jews and Christians can be broken down? That seems to me to be very important.*

S. The Church's hierarchy still doesn't really know what the Church has done throughout its history against the Jews. I remember giving a lecture during the Second Vatican Council in connection with that declaration about the Jews and several cardinals commented afterwards: But the Church has done nothing against the Jews!

That was in 1964–65. Jansen's book may well make a useful contribution to this question. Christians have first to be made aware of all the pronouncements made against the Jews by the Church and then, and then only, can guilt be confessed. Those at the very top of the Church, however, apparently do not know the facts.

O. *They don't want to know them, in my opinion.*

S. Perhaps they don't.

O. *They are perhaps politically difficult to swallow.*

S. Yes. What sort of political attitude — Church politics, I mean — lies behind the fact that the Roman Catholic Church has still not recognized the state of Israel? It is obviously quite impossible, after all, to confess guilt without recognizing the state of Israel and without at the same time accepting further guilt because the problem of the Palestinians has been neglected for so long.

The attitude expressed by the leaders of the Church towards the Jews is, I think, based on a transference on the part of the Church of the unique character of Jesus to itself and to the pope. But Jesus is first and foremost the 'unique one' of Israel.

6

The Bible and man's heart say the same thing

O. *You believe, then, that in practice the Roman Catholic Church has been harmful and even destructive in its attitude towards Judaism. Do you also think the Church has betrayed what was made visible in Jesus Christ?*

S. You have touched here on a problem of fundamental importance. According to the Second Vatican Council, the Church is the 'universal sacrament of salvation'. In its concrete attitude and in its leadership, however, the Church is many times failing to be that sacrament of salvation. It hardly bears prophetic witness to Jesus, but invests itself with royal power. It continues to place almost exclusive emphasis on the exalted Jesus who sits in power because its own authority is apparently increased in this way.

O. *So you think the Church is not in practice the 'sacrament of salvation', but rather an obstacle to salvation?*

S. Yes, I am bound to admit you are right.

O. *When did the Church, in your opinion, first become recognizable in its practical function of bearing witness to the story of the God of Israel, the God who wants justice, and the story of Jesus who is the unique figure of that justice?*

S. I would say from the end of the fourth century onwards. Most people speak of the Emperor Constantine in this context and point to the beginning of the fourth century, but I think that is too early. Christianity certainly became a 'permitted religion', a *religio licita*, alongside Judaism and other religions at that time, but it did not become a state religion then.

That did not happen until the end of the fourth century, during the reign of Emperor Theodosius. It was then that the confession of faith that the second Person of the Trinity became one of us became a law of the Empire and that views that differed from this, such as those held by the Arians, became punishable offences. To begin with, this imperial law was applied in a very flexible way and there were no persecutions as a direct result of its not being observed. In the long run, however, it had enormous consequences. The Roman concept *religio* — in other words, religion as the most important civil commandment and as the pre-eminent civil virtue, veneration of the gods acting as a guarantee of the salvation of the people — was taken over by Christianity! This resulted in a close bond between the Church and the powers of this world, which in turn led to the Church doing the very opposite to bearing witness to the gospel and what is said in that gospel about the kingdom of God. In the Middle Ages especially, the Church underpinned society and acted as a guarantee for it.

O. *Would you say the Roman Catholic Church is still functioning in that way today?*

S. Not only the Roman Catholic Church — many other churches as well! Although, of course, because of its structure, the Roman Catholic Church is much more obviously in that situation than the reformed churches. At the same time, however, there are many local churches and basic communities of Christians who, in their liturgical celebrations and their criticism of society, which is not simply theoretical, but also practical, act as landmarks where the original story of God and Jesus can be recognized. They also act as magnets, attracting all kinds of people who have left the official churches and others who may not be Christians at all, but who encounter authentic community experience in these basic communities. They are usually ecumenical and consist of people of all kinds and all shades of opinion. But these people certainly form a genuine community and one that is fully in keeping with the gospel and even before they are properly aware of it, they are part of the living Judaeo-Christian tradition.

O. *But if that is the case, surely the Bible ought to be dissociated from the Church? If it isn't, will it not be impossible for it to be recognized in the future as a document with something essential and authoritative to say about man's existence? This is, I think, an important question.*

S. I would put it differently. I regard the Bible as a document of the Church, as a datum existing within the community of believers. We have already spoken about this, haven't we? The Christian community existed before the New Testament was written, although, of course, the Old Testament was the written record of an already existing community of believers. The Second Vatican Council placed great emphasis on that fact. And even Lutheran theologians such as Willi Marxsen in his study of the *New Testament as the Church's book* do not say that the Bible is normative outside the Church, as Luther himself did.

To begin with, then, there was a Christian community and those believers recognized themselves in certain Christian writings. They made a selection of those documents — there were, of course, many more Christian texts in circulation in those days than the few that have been included in the New Testament. What is important to remember, however, is that it was not until that time that the New Testament became the ultimate criterion.

According to the Second Vatican Council, even the Church's *magisterium* or teaching office is subject to the Word of God as expressed in the Bible. So you simply cannot take the Bible out of the Church. What you can do is to subject the Church to the criticism of the Bible and the Church has to renew itself again and again throughout history on the basis of that biblical criticism, because again and again the Church takes up a position that is outside the Bible. That is why the basic communities are right to go on criticizing the official churches. The members of those communities have discovered the Bible for themselves and have heard what it says and have continued to listen to it.

All the same, when I hear people saying 'I can't go on with the official Church. The Bible is trampled underfoot in it. I have to leave' well, I can understand how they feel. I certainly do not exclude that possibilty.

O. *More and more people are leaving for that reason. But you exclude that as a possible course of action for yourself, at least for the present?*

S. I have often been asked why I do not leave the Church. People say: your written ideas and your actions are in conflict — even contradictory.

I have two replies to make to this. The first is pragmatical. If all those who criticize the Church leave it, the anti-biblical tendencies in the Church will simply be strengthened. What 'Rome' would have liked most of all, I suspect, is that Hans Küng had become a Protestant. He didn't and was excluded as a Catholic theologian. But he continues as a Catholic and is a thorn in the flesh of the Catholic Church. My second reply to your question is based on my theological standpoint: the Bible and the Church belong together.

O. *So that is your reason for not leaving the Church?*

S. Yes. Despite everything, the Church is the community of God, although that community is very heavily concealed. And a 'pure Church', well, that is from the human and Christian point of view a heresy.

H. *So far, we have talked a great deal about the 'Bible' and it is certainly regarded as a critical element both with regard to the Church and within the Church itself. Why, then, is the Bible so unique? Franz Rosenzweig has told us why he thought the Bible was different from all other books. You can get to know other books, he said, by reading them, but there are two ways of getting to know what is in the Bible. You can hear what it is saying and you can listen to the beating of the human heart. The Bible and man's heart say the same thing. It is for that reason — and only for that reason — that the Bible is 'revelation'. Would you agree with Rosenzweig here?*

S. Yes, I would say the same. You can only believe today if your own human experience tallies with what you find described in the Bible. Believing on authority has just not been possible since the Enlightenment.

O. *Scripture has to tally with the beating of your own heart. What would you say are the preconditions for that? How do you reach the point where you can say, in the modern world: I can recognize my own life and experience in that story?*

S. The most important precondition is that I should discover the really fundamental aspects of my own life and those of society in the story of the Bible in all their depths and heights. The Bible provides me with an answer to my humanity and that answer contains not only a real zest for living, but also the misery of life.

H. *An answer?*

S. Yes, an answer in the sense of hope. In the Bible, we encounter people who take sides and yet are disinterested in their commitment to the poor and oppressed and who do this in order to establish God's justice. But they are themselves cheated in the process. Jesus was crucified for it. Seen from the purely human point of view, his proclamation of the kingdom of God was a failure. It was cancelled out by the powers of his own time. Yet it continued throughout history! A powerful reason for hope! I am confronted with that model of life, that model of human history in the Bible.

And it is an existential confrontation, in other words, it is directly related to what is taking place in my own life and in society.

H. *So there are two poles — the Bible and our situation today. Those two poles are very closely connected. Would you say that one of those two poles acts as the norm or criterion for the other?*

S. No, it is not possible to use just one of those poles as the criterion. Karl Barth used the Bible as his criterion. Friedrich Schleiermacher, with his liberal theology, used the contemporary situation at least to some extent as his criterion. But both of them missed the mark, I think. The one source of revelation, in other words, the criterion, consists in keeping the two poles together in a mutual and critical correlation. The criterion cannot be objectivized in the Bible. As it exists there, objectively, the Bible has no authority. It is only in our interpretation of it in the light of our present situation that the Bible has authority.

H. *Why is the source of revelation to be found in the correlation between the Bible and our present situation?*

S. Because the Bible is itself a so-called 'local theology'. In other words, God brings about salvation in history and that salvation is universal. But salvation for all people can only be found in the particular history of the Jewish people and of Jesus, for example. Jews and Christians express that salvation as a theme in their own cultural forms. Salvation itself, however, is achieved by God in history. That same salvation is also expressed as a theme in local communities at the present time and a contemporary local theology comes about as the result of this. I would make a comparison between the local theology or rather, the local theologies — since there are several of them — of the Bible with the local theologies that are being developed at the present time, just as you could compare Augustine's theology with that of Thomas Aquinas or Luther. The local theologies of the Bible, considered simply on their own, have no greater value than the theologies of our own period.

O. *Do you therefore think there is no such thing as a 'primacy of the Bible'?*

S. There is a primacy of the Bible, yes, but it cannot be 'objectivized'. Strictly speaking, the Word of God is not in the 'letter' of the Bible, nor is it in the 'spirit' of the community reading the Bible. It is in the mutual and living relationship that exists between the two. And that can never be fully objectivized.

H. *You were saying that the Bible itself is a 'local theology'. But you have also said it is a story that concerns all people. Why is that?*

S. Because the essence of the gospel is that man's affair is God's affair and God's affair must become man's affair.

H. *The 'story of liberation', as it is told in the Bible — is it not firmly attached to the basic words, structures and terminology of the Bible?*

S. No, otherwise it would not be a universal story. It certainly comes to us in Jewish and Hellenistic forms. That is the framework within which it is clothed. But it is not 'firmly attached' to that framework. It is transcultural.

O. *Just as you, for example, are not firmly attached to your Roman Catholicism, to the fact that you are Flemish, to the fact that you are a man and sixty-seven years old?*

S. You have to transcend those particular factors in one way or another.

H. *But doesn't it become an abstraction then?*

S. No, on the contrary! That is the great difference between the universal nature of the story of liberation and the universality propagated by the Enlightenment. The Enlightenment philosophers were concerned, for example, with abstract human rights, divorced from a particular culture. The consequence of this was that other cultures, those that were not Western European, were not taken seriously into account. That fact emerged quite clearly in colonization, which began towards the end of the Enlightenment. Universality became totalitarian!

It is very important not to remove the Bible, however universal and transcultural it may be, from its soil, that is, its culture and everything that belongs to that culture, whether it is social, economic or political. If that *is* done, what comes about is an ideology. One culture is made absolute and there is no encounter between different cultures.

Some time ago, when my ideas about this subject were altogether too intellectual, I was of the opinion that the gospel should be translated into new cultural languages and adapted to new cultural circumstances. But you never have the gospel without its cultural soil and you always have that encounter between cultures for that reason.

One of the results of this is the emergence of new theologies. Western European theology is not the only possible theology. For a long time, we believed that it was and this led us to destroy other cultures, with the result that there was no real encounter, but only export. A good example of encounter today is the mutual influence that exists between certain European theologies and the Latin American theology of liberation. To begin with, the Western theologies — and especially the work of Johann Baptist Metz — influenced Latin America. Now, however, there is a reverse trend and the liberation theology of Latin America is having a fruitful effect on European theology. This kind of encounter, which includes mutual recognition and criticism, leads to communion and a community of faith.

7

The great Christian tradition

H. *We have just been talking about the relationship between the Bible and our present historical situation and in the course of that conversation you mentioned the Protestant theologian Karl Barth. One of the major themes in his theology, an aspect in which he showed himself to be representative of the whole tradition of the Reformation, is his attempt to safeguard what is often called, in the traditional terminology, the 'gospel of God's free grace'.*

You have clearly drawn attention to other emphases that contrast quite sharply with that sola scriptura *of the Protestant tradition, without losing sight of the critical function of the Bible. I would very much like to discuss at greater depth your views about the work of theologians who are writing within a different tradition. To what extent is there, do you think, a connection between your theology and that of Ter Schegget, Berkhof or Miskotte?*

S. I ought to point out to begin with how nice I find it that Kuitert, Berkhof and other Protestant theologians describe what I am doing as 'transconfessional theology'. Most of the members of the committee responsible for awarding the Erasmus Prize are theologians working in the tradition of the Reformation and they also called my work 'transconfessional'. Of course, they were aware of my Catholic background — especially in my book *Ministry* on office in the Church — but my two great books on Christology, *Jesus, an Experiment in Christology* and *Christ, the Christian Experience in the Modern World*, they also recognized that my arguments were not based on my Catholic confession, but that I took the great Christian tradition and especially the Old and New Testaments as my point of departure. It would not be wrong to say that I am, in all my recent writing, always listening for an echo of the gospel, whether it is in the churches of the Reformation, the Syrian Church, the Monophysites or the Catholic tradition. I imagine that is why those books have been read by Anglicans and Presbyterians, for example, as much as by Catholics. It has been said in the United States that my theology is for this reason 'post-ecumenical'.

O. *From your own vantage-point as a 'transconfessional theologian', how do you see the other churches?*

S. My inspiration, in my view of the other churches, has always been the Dogmatic Constitution of the Church, *Lumen Gentium*, of the Second Vatican Council. That document doesn't commence with the Roman Catholic Church — oh no, at the very beginning, in the first chapter, the Church is described in biblical images as the 'mystery'. It is only further on in the Constitution that the question is asked: Where is the Church, that vision of being a Church, to be found? In answer to that question, the Constitution says that mystery is in the first place to be found in the Roman Catholic Church, but adds: in a concealed manner!

H. *Is a word such as 'concealed' used?*

S. The text has the word *subsistit in*. Mgr Philips, who wrote most of the text of *Lumen Gentium*, however, said quite explicitly that that was the meaning. There is, after all, the description *sub umbris* as well, pointing to the fact that the Council thought the mystery of the Church was only present in a 'shadowy' form and not in a completely clear and sharp outline.

O. *And is that mystery also in the other churches?*

S. It is present in the other churches, but — and this is what the conciliar teaching amounts to — in an even more concealed form.

O. *Do you agree with that?*

S. There is a different kind of concealment in the case of the other churches, I would say. The authoritarian and hierarchical structure that is so characteristic of the Roman Catholic Church is, of course, not present to such a degree in the other churches.

H. *So would you say that, as far as that is concerned, the other churches are less 'shadowy'?*

S. Yes, I would. But that doesn't mean those churches are not in one way or another one-sided. The Catholic Church and the churches of the Reformation have become isolated from each other and that, of course, is why they have gone their own ways and have become one-sided. Protestants are also looking for possibilities to overcome the one-sided emphases of Luther and Calvin. But it is not an easy search, because the religious separation has also become a cultural separation in the course of history. That is quite obvious from the differences in linguistic usage.

I have experienced this difficulty personally in the meetings I have attended, about four or five times each year, of the central committee for ecumenical relationships. There are, of course, both Catholic and Protestant theologians on that committee. I have several times suddenly felt, during the theological discussions, that I was a total stranger! Miskotte or Van Ruler, for example, may have used a word unknown to Catholics, but apparently of enormous importance to people in the Reformed tradition!

But that sort of experience is really only incidental. It is part of the folklore of the meetings we have together. When it comes to the point, in other words, when it comes to believing in God, in Jesus or in the Church, well, I am not conscious of any factors at all that might divide us as 'Church'. Differences can and must exist, after all, within a single great Church. Those differences are not hard to find even in the Roman Catholic Church.

H. *You have described your own theology as 'transconfessional'. Have you observed similar theological projects in the tradition of the Protestant Reformation as well?*

S. There is less evidence of 'transconfessional' theology in Protestant circles. The confessional background is still quite marked in the work of Berkhof and Kuitert, for example. It is also noticeably present in the case of Ter Schegget.

O. *All the same, you would recognize them as brothers in their proclamation of the gospel?*

S. Yes.

H. *You have just said: When it comes to the point, there are no more real differences. But we noticed while we were talking about Scripture that your emphases were different from those of Karl Barth, for example, or those who have followed him and gone further than him. Let me try to be a little more precise by* *quoting from Miskotte. In his book on the 'silence of the gods' —* Als de goden zwijgen *— he says: 'Even though we are bound to take ourselves as our point of departure in every "sphere" in which revelation and faith are discussed, we cannot really take ourselves as our point of departure. We have to make a more precise distinction. We can say, for example, using the word in a good sense, that faith has its own kind of autonomy, that it is personal, that it is chosen in freedom and that the Word of God has authority of a kind that not only brings about freedom, but also, enclosed within itself, entails freedom, creates it and sustains it. But there must be a place "somewhere" where the criterion of the truth is not to be found with me. There must be a "somewhere" where man can say in the absolute sense that he is not lonely, that he is not alone and neither a creator nor a judge. There must be "somewhere" where he has, less in ecstasy than with a sober sense of what is true, to feel permitted to understand that he is understood and known and that he has been chosen'.*

S. Yes, I can agree with Miskotte there. But only subject to one condition: that this cannot simply be affirmed.

O. *What do you mean by that?*

S. You just can't say: 'That is how it is'. That there is in fact a mystery and that you let that mystery guide your life — you have to let that mystery be seen in one way or another or it will continue to be unintelligible. I think this really touches on the central difference between the Roman Catholic view and that of the Reformation. I would make an exception here of Kuitert, who is, as far as this question is concerned, in the same tradition as myself, but most Protestant theologians and especially those who are working in the tradition of Karl Barth and Miskotte do not fully accept man's autonomy.

What we have here in fact is the old problem of natural theology. In other words, how am I to render an account of my faith? Well, you have above all to let it be seen which moments are the right ones for speaking meaningfully about God and Jesus. And that is even more important now, in the present century, when the religious *a priori* no longer exists and God has become problematical precisely as God. Now that is certainly not a Protestant approach.

O. *What you are saying is that the mystery must be made intelligible. You must provide the context within which it is meaningful to speak about God. Have I understood you correctly? Would you give us an example of what you mean?*

S. Yes, I will. There are, for instance, freedom movements everywhere in the modern world. People everywhere are looking for liberation, for salvation. In the past, salvation seemed to be a theme that was exclusively religious, but now more and more people without explicit religious faith are taking up this theme. You could almost say that every science and sphere of knowledge exists now for the purpose of healing man, of making man and his world whole. Even the socialist movement is concerned with man's healing, his salvation. So, if I want to speak about God in the modern world and I am conscious of the way in which the Judaeo-Christian tradition speaks about God as the liberator, then I can only speak about him, in our world today, in the context of liberation in that world. I have to make it quite clear that God is not present in structures of slavery, where there is no freedom, but that he is present in the struggle of the poor against the injustice that oppresses them. In other words, when I speak the name of God, I name the deepest mystery and the ground of all the movements of liberation that are present in the world today.

H. *What you have just been describing — is it your own development of 'natural theology'?*

S. Yes, it is. In the past, natural theology was principally concerned with providing proofs of the existence of God. It is just not possible to do that now. You can't prove the existence of God. What you can do is to show there are human contexts in which it is more meaningful to use the word 'God' than not to use it. I would call that contemporary natural theology.

H. *In Barth's later theological writings — didn't he also make room, towards the end of his life, for a similar form of natural theology?*

S. Yes, it's true to say there was a development in Barth's thinking in this direction. In the end, however, you are bound to describe his theology, as Bonhoeffer did, as a positivism of revelation.

O. *What does that mean?*

S. It means that God's Word descends vertically from heaven into the Bible, without involving man's experience at all. And I have to let myself be guided by the authority of that Word, whether it has any real meaning for me or not. You have to listen to it, because 'that is how it is'. I sometimes listen to sermons on the radio given by Protestants and I am conscious of the grim tone used to address listeners. And the less the message appeals to people, the grimmer the tone becomes.

So I have to ask myself: How did 'God's Word' in the Bible come about? Surely people wrote it down! God didn't 'speak' it. Men made God speak and always because of concrete events. God's Word itself is a metaphor.

H. *Karl Barth himself said: Everything I say about God I say as a man about God.*

S. Yes, as a man. But I would add to that: inspired by what has taken place in history, by God in people. The people of Israel interpreted their own history as a history of liberation by God. That interpretation is included in the Bible.

O. *So there are experiences of liberation, in people and between people. Liberation has taken place and those experiences are named. Then it is said — as Van Peursen calls it — 'It is him again'. We attribute it to God.*

S. Yes, that's right: It is him again. Thus speaks Yhwh! But it is believers who say that — those who believe in Yhwh. In other words, revelation does not come from my experience as such. It is not the product of my experience. Miskotte is right in that. And in that sense, I agree with Barth in his reaction to the liberal theologians, who took contemporary experiences as their criterion for interpreting Scripture. But Barth, of course, went too far in the other direction. I think in terms of a critical confrontation between the gospel and the modern world.

O. *People have experiences of liberation with themselves and each other and then say: 'It is him again'. What do they really mean by attributing it to God? Has he really liberated us? Do they mean: He has liberated us or you have liberated yourselves? Or do they mean: You are in a position to be able to rescue yourself? Or you are once again in that position? Perhaps you could say we save ourselves because the power, the ability to set ourselves free has been given to us by God?*

S. Yes, that's how I see it, I think. I don't think there is any opposition between saving oneself and God's grace. During the Reformation, the two came to be seen as quite distinct from each other, but I am sure there is only one reality. People try to help each other and to set each other free and what they have in mind is the well-being of all men. People do that themselves. Those who believe also see it as God's saving activity. But God never acts outside of men and women.

O. *You made a connection a little while ago between natural theology and the liberation movements that exist in such numbers in the world today. The Dutch Reformed theologian, Bert ter Schegget, has become very well known in the Netherlands for the special contribution he has been making to a theology of liberation. In this, he has, of course, to some extent been following in the footsteps of Barth and Miskotte. Certainly many members of the movement are aware of the part he has been playing. What is your attitude towards his theology?*

S. I am in agreement with most of what he is saying, but at the same time I have to criticize him for being too inclined to take a religious *a priori* as his point of departure. That can be attributed, of course, to the influence of Karl Barth. But it is simply no longer possible to assume a religious *a priori* in our secularized Western society. That is why I think his theology of liberation is in danger of becoming an ideology.

H. *Is a 'messianic ideology' not possible, then?*

S. I would not want to accept that possibility quite so quickly. I am very conscious, for example, of Jesus as the 'anti-Messiah' when I read the New Testament. What I mean is that Jesus is not the Messiah as we imagine him or the Messiah that we would like to see. We should take this into account in the liberation that we ourselves bring about. In any case, I would certainly not want to expose myself to a Marxist form of neo-dogmatism and whenever I am aware of that particular ideology among my students I oppose it very firmly. I have suffered too much myself from dictatorship in the Church and have become distinctly allergic to every form of dogmatism, no matter where it comes from. That doesn't mean, of course, that I think you cannot be a Christian and a Marxist at the same time. But you have to have a critical attitude both towards Christianity and towards Marxism.

I am myself very strongly drawn towards a Christian form of socialism, but I would never claim that that is the only way of being a Christian. I am hopeful too that the theology of liberation and the liberation movement will not decline into ideology. The freedom movement in Nicaragua is, I think, going in the right direction. The freedom that has already been achieved there — it would seem that they want to continue in the same direction. As long as they don't fail! There are already signs of dictatorship here and there.

O. *Those dictatorial attitudes are forced on the people, wouldn't you agree, by the presence of American capital?*

S. Yes, of course. Their freedom is threatened again and again. The great problem, as I see it, is therefore what happens after the revolution. How do you deal with the counter-forces that inevitably try to smash the freedom you have already achieved and want to make it almost impossible for the revolution to succeed without once again sliding imperceptibly into a dictatorship? I haven't found any solution to that problem yet.

O. *If Berkhof, for example, were taking part in this conversation about Protestant theology today, what question would you put to him?*

S. The most important question I would like to ask him and other Protestant theologians is really to do with what I have just said about natural theology. In *Weerwoord*, a collection of essays written in 'response' to Berkhof's book on faith, *Christelijk Geloof*, I contributed an article entitled 'God had a small beginning', which is a statement made by Berkhof himself. My main task in that article was to discuss Berkhof's treatment of natural theology in the introduction to his book, in which he was directly concerned with the relationship between creation and the covenant. Berkhof sees creation very much from the vantage-point of the redemption. I would go along with him, of course, for quite a distance in this. After all, you have to speak about creation within the Judaeo-Christian tradition and not apart from it. But as a Catholic theologian — and my Thomist background plays a part in this — I am bound to see creation as the foundation. It is surely for a very good reason that the Bible opens with the story of creation as the beginning of God's dealing with his creature, human beings, in the covenant. But Berkhof — and other Protestant theologians — stresses the redemption. He seems to be insisting that it is only possible to say anything about creation from the standpoint of the redemption. The result is, then, that, outside the redemption, nature is regarded as *natura corrupta*. Man is a corrupt being. I do not regard man as a corrupt being. I see a great deal of good in him.

O. *Would you say that is a difference in the interpretation of original sin and the fall?*

S. Yes. I know there is something wrong with man, but I still prefer to take the fundamental goodness of creation as my point of departure. That goodness is not cancelled out by man's sin.

O. *What is sin?*

S. Everything that goes against being human.

O. *But Barth said we don't know what being human really is — that has first to be revealed.*

S. I would say what sinfulness in all its depth is and what being human in its sublimity may be — that has been revealed in Jesus. Jesus has revealed God to us and, in that revelation, he has revealed what being human is. But over and against this the fact remains that, as you look around you, there are very many people of high moral character who have nothing whatever to do with religion.

H. *That Protestant view of man does not mean that man cannot be of a high moral character.*

S. Then there must be certain conclusions to be drawn from that.

O. *Ought we not to say that the world, with all its wisdom and all its moral sublimity, was not able to achieve justice for all people? The very opposite seems to have been the case — Jesus, the just man, the embodiment of righteousness, was nailed to the cross!*

S. That is true. Seen from the perspective of man's redemption and of what man might be, everything that does not resemble that vision looks even darker.

H. *Would it not be true to say that redemption, the figure of Jesus of Nazareth, attracts all kinds of different figures of justice, some Christian and some not, into its orbit?*

S. This still does not make me any less wary of the Protestant view, which certainly shows man up in a dark and sombre perspective in order to place Jesus in an even clearer light. I prefer to see man placed on a pedestal, to use the image that occurs in the psalms, in which man thanks God for making him man! The same idea also occurs in some of the Greek Fathers of the Church, such as Irenaeus. They did not share the view, as Augustine did, that man was in a state of original sin.

O. *What was their view of man, then?*

S. They thought man had a small beginning, but grew and became better. Augustine taught that man began at a great height — in paradise. Then he sinned and fell and it was all over with him. Only Jesus was still able to save him. Well, I think that's a gruesome way of thinking, especially when you see how Billy Graham and popular evangelists like him express it. It contains real dangers — it's a threat to our spiritual health and well-being.

O. *Would you say that Augustinian view has always been present in Berkhof's teaching?*

S. Yes, I would, but in his case it is not gruesome. He has integrated it into his own vision in quite a healthy and harmonious way.

O. *But you would insist that the Protestant theologians for the most part refuse to let go of that idea of man as a corrupt being?*

S. No, they won't let go of it. I know, of course, that Thomas Aquinas also spoke about the *vulnera naturae*, the wounds inflicted on our human nature. But his teaching was really quite different. Our human history undoubtedly has demonic aspects, but it is important to go on looking at the good that has always taken place in that history and is still taking place in it, even outside the sphere of Christianity. You can certainly make a connection between that good and Jesus, but if you do that you are interpreting it in the light of your own convictions. A Buddhist can say, in the same way, about a Christian: he is an 'anonymous Buddhist'.

H. *If you look at Protestant theology in that way, can you really go on believing that your own theology is transconfessional? It strikes me that it is typically Catholic — and I don't mean Catholic in the purely negative sense. Surely 'transconfessional' means something quite different, doesn't it?*

S. If by transconfessional you mean a theology that is above or outside all Christian confessions, then it must be a pure abstraction and therefore a theology that no authentic Christian theologian could ever teach. It would also not be sound theology — no one can ever think or believe from no point of view at all. What does 'ecumenical' mean, after all, in this context? Does it not mean that we have to bear in mind the great Christian tradition that can be found in all the Christian churches — the *Catholica*, which does not in itself coincide with the empirical phenomenon of the Roman Catholic Church? In that sense, my work is, I think, a valid contribution to the unity of the churches, in which there may be all kinds of differences, but in which the one Church community recognizes itself in the other communities and they recognize themselves in it.

8

The feminist movement and the peace movement

O. *What is the significance of the feminist movement for you?*

S. The third book in my Christological trilogy, the one that will follow *Jesus, an Experiment in Christology* and *Christ, the Christian Experience*, will be a western theology of liberation. I shall be discussing the feminist theology in it, since that clearly has a place there. It is, of course, a very typical form of Western European and American liberation theology. The Latin American theologians are fighting shy of it, I feel, because the women's liberation movement in Latin America is functioning rather differently there from the way in which it is functioning here. If the wives of the big landowners are struggling for emancipation there, they are going against their own theology of liberation, which is, of course, a theology of and for the poor. Those are the kind of reactions that I hear and I can understand them. But the people there will get over them, I don't doubt.

O. *What, in your opinion, is the most important impulse coming at the moment from the feminist theology?*

S. The feminist theologians are providing evidence of a fundamental process of emancipation among women — a process of which we were hardly aware ten years ago. There have in fact been so many books and articles published that I have myself come to think much more feminist-ically and I am much more conscious of the levels at which discrimination is practised against women in the whole of society and in the whole of the Church. Feminist theologians are themselves making us conscious of this.

O. *A feminist theologian, Maria de Groot, said recently: It must all be re-thought* *and rewritten — the whole dogmatic teaching of the Church, all the Church's exegesis, all the historiography of the Church, everything, because all that theology is concerned with is wholeness and so far all that we have had is half, the male half. What is your opinion of that kind of statement?*

S. I have a great deal of sympathy for it. It can't be denied that our cultures are male cultures and our philosophies and theologies are those of men. Male domination is clearly expressed in our language about God. But we shall not find a solution by saying 'she' instead of 'he' when we speak about God or calling God 'Mother' instead of 'Father'.

O. *I suppose there are really more ways of solving this problem than those that have been used up till now. Maria de Groot thinks the most important question is whether the feminine is good enough and whether it is regarded as worthy to designate the divine.*

S. That is right, of course.

O. *Words like heart, lap, womb, breath and light — these are also biblical images for the divine. There is, in the Bible, a level of image or metaphorical language that is much more open than the level at which words such as father and son are used and it is also less concerned with the specific elements of the male cultural environment. In those words 'father' and 'son', for example, a contrast is always evoked. By this I mean when you hear 'father', you also hear: 'father, not mother' and when you hear 'son', you hear 'son, not daughter'. Dante's verse about God: 'Love that moves the sun and the stars' is more open than 'Creator of heaven and earth' and for that reason it may be more suitable for a new liturgical language.*

S. There are points of contact in the language of the Bible that we have still not discovered. Isaiah, for example, describes God in maternal images.

H. *Would you say our one-sided and male way of describing God is derived from the cultural and social context within which the Bible was written? We have already talked about this in another context, you may remember. If that is so, it ought to be possible to 'translate' it.*

S. Yes, it can be translated, I am sure.

H. *The unique message of Scripture is, in other words, not distinctively 'male'.*

S. No, certainly not. The Bible came about in a male culture, of course, and I don't object to the fact that that is how it is in the Bible — that revelation came to us at that moment in our history in just that way and that manner of speaking. But it would be wrong if *we* were to think and speak about woman in the same way. In my view, we should not try to change those words and images in the Bible. We should rather try to emancipate ourselves. Woman must be given another place in our society.

O. *Should that be expressed, do you think, in the language we use about God, a language that is not the same as that of the Bible. And if it were, would it enrich that language?*

S. Yes, I think it would. But that will only come about if women fight for it. And men must also join women in their fight against suppression. If I understand them correctly, what the feminist theologians have done is to trace and discover the fundamental error in Western theology since Augustine especially. The sin of pride, which is, of course, the principal sin, has always been seen as a sinful preoccupation with self-assertion. This has made us blind to the fact that the female preoccupation with self-denial was imposed on women by consciously and unconsciously living in the sexist and patriarchal structures of society and the Church. Those structures forced women to deny themselves in the name of what was in fact an un-Christian understanding both of pride and of self-sacrifice. The dominant doctrine in the Church of sin and grace encouraged women to be passive and to overlook themselves. Now the feminist theologians have come to understand that an authentic doctrine of sin and grace must include the idea of responsible self-assertion on the part of women with and for others, an idea that, if made a reality, is liberating.

The earlier theology was, on the one hand, a reflection of the social and economic structures that in fact existed. On the other hand, however, it also stabilized and strengthened those structures. That is why it is not difficult to distinguish two broad tendencies in feminist theology. On the one hand, there is a movement which tries to expose the elements that are present in the whole of theology and that discriminate against women. On the other, there is a tendency which is directly concerned with the task of analysing the socio-economic structures that underlie discrimination against women.

The first of these two movements consists for the most part of American feminist theologians, who are principally concerned with a change of attitude towards women in the Church and a change in the way of thinking and speaking about women. These theologians are therefore above all preoccupied with the Bible and with the traditional teaching of the

Church. They are, for example, very concerned with hostile statements made about women in the writings of the Church Fathers.

In the Netherlands, on the other hand, feminist theologians tend to follow a different direction. They are less orientated towards women and their position in the Church and far more concerned with the place of women in society, although that includes the Church, since the Church has simply taken over the prevailing social structures. The feminist theologians of this broad tendency are first and foremost critical of society and culture.

O. *To what degree is that theology?*

S. It is often, of course, primarily critical sociology, in this case directed towards the liberation of women. But it can become theology. What is sometimes called 'theology that is critical of society' is often no more than a repetition, applied to women, of what sociologists have to say in general critical terms. It can only be called theology in the strict sense of the word when it forms part of a theological project and is, for example, an attempt to answer the question: How should the forms within which revelation has come to us be reshaped, at least as far as certain aspects are concerned, so that a perpetuation in theology of discrimination against women can be avoided?

It is clear from very many books and articles that have been recently published that feminist theology is still in the process of being formed. It is still very much concerned, often in great detail, with the purely negative experience of discrimination and we men are, of course, not yet fully aware of those negative details. I am bound to say the feminist theologians are right in their attempt to analyse and explain those details, but I am at the same time also bound to ask whether theology will be fundamentally changed by that attempt. My answer to this question is, I think, yes, it will, at the level of our response to theology far more fundamentally than at the level of systematic or thematic treatment of theological questions. I think the whole of theology will come to be seen in a different light, but I cannot tell whether the feminist theologians themselves believe that will happen or not.

I spent a year recently supervising a theological project on the subject of 'woman' and I learned a great deal from it. I often felt that what the students were doing had nothing to do with feminist theology, but when I came to analyse their work more closely, I began to recognize they were right. The general attitude of the Roman Catholic Church is, I am afraid, still fundamentally that the woman's place is in the home, in the kitchen and with her family.

What lies behind that attitude? What is involved here is, I think, the patriarchal pattern of life of people living in rural areas. After all, all the great religions are rural religions. They all originated in an agrarian culture and those who belonged to them were country dwellers. How can a religion that is conditioned by that agrarian origin be transferred to the modern world — a world in which women are struggling to be liberated? What an enormous project!

I have never worked directly at any feminist theological project, although I have read a great deal about feminism and feminist theology and have read many works by American and Dutch feminists. I have certainly become more sensitive to the problem. I have also become sensitive to the language and the images used. Once, during a conference, I compared the Church to a decrepit old woman and the feminists present reacted violently to this image, which comes, of course, from the Shepherd of Hermas. I shan't use it again!

O. *Is there one particular circle of Roman Catholic theologians within which you feel completely at home? The editorial board of* Concilium, *for example?*

S. *Concilium* is certainly a very unusual phenomenon — an international theological journal, appearing ten times a year, the same text in seven different languages and about thirty thousand copies printed. It was the brainchild of the Dutch publisher Paul Brand. He was convinced, as early as 1958, of the need to break through the isolation that existed between various schools of theology and even then had plans for a journal of this kind. When he asked Karl Rahner then, however, Rahner said: 'No, we won't be able to write what we want to'.

Paul Brand relaunched his plan in 1962, during the first session of the Second Vatican Council. Two-thirds of the bishops had just risked rejecting the so-called 'Schema on the Sources of Revelation', a document prepared by Vatican theologians led by Cardinal Ottaviani and the Jesuit Father Tromp, and he thought the time was ripe for an international theological journal as an open forum for theologians all over the world to express their views. He was not wrong! Rahner, Küng and I were already on his side and the first number of *Concilium* appeared in January 1965. Now, almost twenty years later, *Concilium* has become a club of friends — internationally well-known theologians such as Congar, Chenu, David Tracy, Metz and Gutiérrez — and theologians are able to express themselves freely in it and say just what they like. Our relationship with Rome is not very good, of course, and we supported Pohier and Küng when their work was condemned. There is an annual conference where between thirty and forty theologians talk about the themes to be debated in numbers of the following year.

During the years immediately following the Council, we formed a theologically coherent group on the basis of the documents published in the course of the Council. There is a great deal of pluriformity among us now. There are, for example, theologians who say quite openly: I could as well be a Buddhist as a Christian. Once we had a session in which we conducted a kind of examination of conscience lasting a whole day. Each of us was given ten minutes in which to tell the others where we stood, so many years after the Council. It was astonishing how many differences in insight and experience were brought to light — including political views. Hardly anyone voted for a Christian party any more and that was nothing compared with our points of view in Church matters. There was no one, for example, who completely identified himself with the official Church, but at the same time we all recognized each other as deeply convinced believers.

O. *Would it be true to say that you feel yourself to be closer to Johann Baptist Metz as a 'political theologian' than to Hans Küng, who believes you 'can follow Jesus without being politically or socially critically committed'?*

S. Yes, I would say I have very much the same political orientation as Metz. I am on a different wave-length from Küng, however. He is mainly concerned with what is going on inside the Church and not with politics. That is why Metz calls him, in that sense at least, a 'liberal' theologian.

O. *How 'political' are the North American theologians, would you say?*

S. They are for the most part very radical in their criticism of the Reagan administration, for example, but unfortunately they aren't doing very much about it. 'We shall have a dictatorship in the United States in ten years' time' they tell me, but they seem to be so resigned to it! All American intellectuals — indeed everyone I have spoken to in every American university — are sick of Reagan, but hardly any of them are protesting, for example, against the American involvement in El Salvador, although during the Vietnamese war . . . Americans have been softened up . . . They were so humiliated by the results of the Vietnamese war . . . They haven't recovered from that experience yet.

O. *Isn't it time for all the theologians in Europe, North America and the Third World to affirm their commitment to the peace movement by appealing with one voice to all those who call themselves Christians to reject nuclear armament? The majority of Dutch people are probably against nuclear weapons, but in every election there is still a majority vote for parties that do not totally reject nuclear armament. Only recently, the politician Bas de Gaay Fortmann said: 'As a member of the Calvanist Reformed Church in the Netherlands, the last party I would want to vote for is the Communist Party. But if that party was the only party in our country to reject nuclear weapons, then all of us who belong to the Calvanist Reformed Church would have to vote for it. We would have to let our objections to its basic policies go and give priority to its intention to abolish nuclear weapons, because nuclear armament is the greatest of all the evils threatening us at the present time.*

I have only quoted Fortmann because what he says expresses a very striking contrast. Harry Kuitert is a theologian who also belongs to the Dutch Calvanist Reformed Church and you have already said you feel spiritually very close to him in many respects. He has said he thinks the Church ought to remain silent about this issue. But you take a different view, don't you? You have already spoken out in favour of disarmament, haven't you?

Ought theologians and Church leaders not to initiate, in a much less ambiguous way then they have done so far, a process of examination of conscience among Christians, directed quite clearly towards the abolition of nuclear armaments? Would it not be quite justifiable for them to advise members of their churches how to vote in this respect? Or do you think that would be going too far?

S. I was in New York a few weeks ago in the Palace of the United Nations. There was an exhibition there of the atom bomb attacks on Hiroshima and Nagasaki. Photos, bits of clothing, scorched household goods . . . Enough for anyone looking at them to be able to say: Let it never happen again. We are always going to be better off without atom bombs.

This should really form the basis of an ethical protest that puts all other protests in the shade. That is how I look at Bas de Gaay Fortmann's statement. And that is why I simply cannot understand why so many Church leaders are still hesitating to speak out against nuclear weapons.

In the near future there will be a number of *Concilium* devoted to the peace movement and to peace movements generally. It will express the evangelical demand that the abolition of all atomic weapons is the beginning of all disarmament.

I feel that Kuitert's view is not essentially different from this, although he is obviously wary of efforts made to commit the Church to action because of his own political insights. The churches have, after all, often missed the goal when they have joined in the game. I think — and I am with Kuitert here — that the churches have the task not so much of pointing to the concrete (and often ambiguous) means, as of revealing the ideology of 'national safety' by which the armament race is so often justified. This is, I am sure, where the churches have a really prophetic task and one in which they can form the consciences of their members. I would urge the churches to be active in this sphere especially.

I also think, however, in view of the madness of the armaments race at the moment, that the churches ought to go further than this. It would not be wrong for them to declare quite explicitly: 'Gentlemen (for it is above all "gentlemen" who keep the armaments race going), however valuable your arguments for continued armament may be, they are still arguments made within a demonic circle of madness and so we, as the Church of Christ, condemn all nuclear weapons and call on all people to oppose them by every means including political ones'.

9

Critical communities and office in the Church

O. *You say you once compared the Church to a decrepit old woman, but you would never make that comparison again. It's obvious, of course, what you meant by it. How is it possible for anyone still to accept an office in that Church? Do you think there is still any justification for encouraging men to become priests?*

S. If becoming a priest were to mean that a man would simply become a moving part in a hierarchical machine and act as a functionary, unquestioningly carrying out the orders of those in authority in that Church, then I would certainly ask that man: Could you take that step?

O. *But that is what usually happens, isn't it?*

S. That is what often happens, yes, but I think it's also possible to be in the Church and even to hold office in the Church, as a priest, that is, and be constantly aware of the prophetic task and need to criticize the Church again and again in the light of the gospel. That is one of the tasks of the person holding office, after all.

O. *So you think you can choose to hold office in the Church in order to maintain a counter-movement in that Church?*

S. If you hold office, you have the prophetic function of proclaiming the gospel of Jesus, in other words, of proclaiming justice. So, wherever there is injustice, you have to oppose it and that means you have to oppose it first of all in the Church itself. If criticism of the Church were only to come from outside the Church . . . Well, the Church is generally speaking not particularly troubled by that sort of criticism.

O. *So for practical considerations you would say: Let people offer themselves for office in that Church, but let them act as prophets when they hold that office.*

S. No, I wouldn't say that. It wouldn't be simply for practical considerations . . . for reasons of strategy. It goes deeper than that.

O. *If it were just for reasons of strategy, then, you wouldn't insist on it?*

S. No, it isn't just a question of strategy. I would never say, for example: You shouldn't leave the Church just for reasons of strategy or if you leave, you'll get nowhere, but if you stay in the Church and you are critical, you may stimulate it . . . you may still be able to do something positive. No, I think it goes deeper. It is comparable to the relationship between the prophets and Israel. The prophets were always going counter to the established, settled Israelites, criticizing the leaders and the people, but they didn't separate themselves and stand outside Israel. On the contrary! It was from their view of Israel from within that they continued to criticize!

O. *What you would like to see, then, is a priesthood committed to carrying out a prophetic function. Your would then have the wonderful, but up till now very unusual situation in which a person is ordained by the Church's hierarchy in order to go against that hierarchy. What that means in fact is that priests are ordained in order to go into opposition.*

S. Yes, but I look at it this way: It is not primarily a question of the Church. It is above all a question of the gospel of Jesus, on the basis of which people form a community, a Church, with each other. That Church has developed in history in such a way that it has in fact become a power over and against the gospel. But that Church is subject to the criticism of the gospel, just as Israel was subject to the criticism of the prophets. So anyone who has been seized by that gospel, whether he or she is a 'lay' person or in office, is bound to criticize, accuse and attack whatever enslaves people. All those who live the life of the gospel are bound to judge the hierarchy of the Church as a power.

O. *This book containing our conversations may perhaps be bought by people who no longer feel at home in the Church and who have no possibility of criticizing or accusing that power that you have mentioned. The only way they may have of protesting is just to stay away — the silent 'lapsing' that has taken place during the past thirty years or more in the Netherlands and elsewhere. And hardly anyone comes forward now as a candidate for the priesthood! But the bishops are* *still asking us to pray for new vocations. What do you think ought to be done about this?*

S. On the one hand, our bishops are making it impossible for people to come forward as priests, but on the other hand we are asked to pray for priests. That is a falsification — a falsification of what prayer really is as well. Thomas Aquinas had a relevant comment to make here. In one text he said: There are certain matters in which man has such control of himself that he may act completely on his own account, even if this goes against a possible prohibition issued by the pope. In such a case, a papal commandment or prohibition must be seen as wrong. It has *ipso facto* no validity or power. Then in another text, Thomas says: It is sometimes necessary to oppose a papal commandment, even at the risk of being excommunicated. Thomas is clearly relativizing the Church's hierarchy! For him, the highest authorities are the gospel and the human conscience. If the system is functioning properly, the Church acts as a mediator between the two.

The centralization of the Church's power in the Roman structures began in the eleventh century. Luther's and Calvin's criticism of the Church — and the criticism of the whole of the Reformation — didn't just come down from heaven! The Church had identified itself so completely with a Christ it had made into an absolute ruler — a misrepresentation of Christ, in other words — that it had in fact become a power structure, an institution that was removed from the criticism of the gospel. Those encyclicals written during the nineteenth century, for example, transferring the power of Christ directly and almost unreflectingly to the pope — they were terribly mistaken. And the same thing is happening again under the present pope!

O. *How do you feel yourself in this Church, under this pope?*

S. I have learned a great deal from my study of history. Supreme responsibility becomes tyranny in the hands of men, even in the Church. But even that aspect can be relativized! I am conscious of a counter-movement at work that has never been completely silenced throughout two thousand years of Christianity. The prophetic voice has always been audible in the Church.

O. *You have become more and more of a spokesman of that counter-movement in the course of your life, haven't you?*

S. Yes, more and more, that's true. And that's because I have become more and more conscious of the disastrous way in which the power structures have become consolidated in the Church. There was to some extent at least a breakthrough for the first time at the Second Vatican Council, I think.

O. *I have the impression that the Second Vatican Council was really a bit of everything mixed with everything else. I suppose we can say that now, but the two so-called 'conservative' Dutch Catholic bishops, Gijsen and Simonis, are still typical exponents of the Council — or aren't they?*

S. They are not.

O. *But they are always appealing to the Second Vatican Council — almost as if they are the only ones who interpret the conciliar texts reliably.*

S. Bishop Gijsen is always appealing to certain texts, you might say very special ones. Many bishops do that. An Italian theologian put all the quotations from Vatican II into a computer and the computer told him that those bishops were quoting the Second Vatican Council in those places where it was quoting from Vatican I. I am sure the great weakness of Vatican II was that it compromised with Vatican I.

O. *You have just quoted a striking text of Thomas Aquinas. Have you always been inspired by his teaching?*

S. I read that text ten years ago and it struck me particularly then and gave me encouragement. But it is only in recent years that it has really come alive for me.

O. *When did you first become aware of the fact that you ought to play a part in the counter-movement you spoke about a moment ago? During the Second Vatican Council?*

S. No, long before that. Even before 1957, when I was teaching in Louvain, I was quite critical of the official theology of the Church in my own theology. I was very influenced in those days in my reaction to the Roman theology by Rahner and Congar. But after the Second Vatican Council and especially when the reactionary forces in the Church paralyzed all progress — that was from about 1969 or 1970 onwards — it became not just a theological question for me, but a really existential question: How should I proceed?

I looked around and saw various critical communities emerging in the

Church. That was decisive for me. A marginal critical movement that was nonetheless spreading throughout the whole Church. I wanted to go along with that movement and, as it were, supervise it theologically, because I realized the future of the Church was in it. If the Church is ever to change at the top, I thought, it has to recognize that it is in fact becoming more and more a top without a base — the base, that is, people themselves, have gone their own way. It is only in this way that the top can change. And it will change!

O. *Do you have sympathy with those people who say: The Roman Catholic Church (and perhaps all the established churches as well) is obviously not functioning any more. It is no longer mediating salvation. So we can no longer play any part in that Church.*

S. I can accept that. There must be schisms — that is an old saying. And those are often providential ways. What can we say about God's intention with his Church? It is all a question of history. So you see that, when there have been schisms, the Church really is 'converted', reformed — sometimes years, sometimes centuries later. The Second Vatican Council achieved, at least partly, what the Reformation wanted to achieve in the fifteenth and sixteenth centuries.

H. *Do you think the Church has learned anything from this experience in the course of history?*

S. Yes, slowly, but it has learned. The emergence of the critical communities I have mentioned is evidence of that — they have emerged from the great, slow Church.

O. *In ordinary language, the word 'Church' is used, sometimes without the capital letter of course, for both — that 'great, slow Church' and the 'critical Church', 'basic church communities', 'grass-roots church' or what have you. Wouldn't it be better to make a clear distinction between each?*

S. In the New Testament, the word *ecclesia* is used sometimes for the great *oikoumene*, but whenever it occurs in the Pauline letters it means the church in Corinth, the church in Thessalonica or whatever.

O. *The local church, then, the* ecclesia *in Corinth, the* ecclesia *or the church in Thessalonica — that is really what is involved? That is the most important 'church'?*

S. Yes, that is the church of first importance — the critical community in Ijmond or in Schaesberg or in Kampen or wherever. That has always been the most important church or Christian community. But there is another important aspect to this question. There is evidence in the New Testament of conflict between, for example, the Johannine community and the community of Peter. And then we have an allusion to this in the gospel of John: 'In my Father's house there are many rooms'. This means, of course, that there are also Petrine and Pauline communities alongside the Johannine community. And then Jesus prays for the unity of those churches in the same gospel. What does this mean? It means the emphasis can be different in the various local churches and there can be a really pluralistic movement, but they are all fundamentally joined to the one — to Jesus.

I agree that it is good that the local church of Rome has a leader, its bishop, who has the function of Peter and ultimately sees to it that there is unity between the other local churches. But that is the only function of the church of Rome — to be a kind of appeal court, so that, in the last resort, the local churches can make an appeal to that Petrine office.

In recent centuries, the local church has been almost entirely subjected to the power of the pope. He has decided almost everything. He has appointed the bishops and that is of critical importance. Because of this, the real needs and the possibilities of the local churches have often been misunderstood and their real saving power has been seriously restricted. There have been times and circumstances when this restriction has possibly operated well, but now it has become a system of coercion that must be broken. The local churches — we call them 'critical communities' in the Netherlands when they are functioning as they should — must inevitably play a very important part in that process, that breakthrough. As far as I am concerned, it is not the top in Rome that is of first importance — it is the local community.

O. *Jan Nieuwenhuis, the pastor in the Dominicus community in Amsterdam, asked a woman who belonged to that community recently whether she had any question to put to you. This is her question: 'Does the celebration of the Eucharist without an ordained priest, by a lay person, have the same value as it did in the past? Is a celebration with a lay person leading really a celebration of the Eucharist? And if it is, why are there still ordinations?' It hardly needs to be said what the top functionaries in the Dutch Church would reply to this question. What is your reply?*

S. People ask questions of this kind quite legitimately on the basis of the criticism that the basic communities can make of the top in Rome. If the

Church were functioning normally, that is, from the base upwards, no one would ever think of letting a 'lay person' lead in the Eucharist.

O. *Do you mean that the person leading in the celebration, whether it is a man or a woman, would therefore no longer be a 'lay person'?*

S. A whole complex of functions and offices has come about, a sociological structure, in the course of history when the Church was being formed and the community was being built up. The community lives, however, in the light of a datum that it has not created itself — the inspiration, the spirit of Jesus of Nazareth, in whom it has recognized the Messiah. That man from Nazareth is the norm of the whole of that 'Church' movement. The community has to take care to remain in the spirit of Jesus of Nazareth — the whole community. Then you see — and that is a sociological datum — that what the whole of the community has to do becomes a specialization in certain cases, with the task of activating or inspiring the community so that the community will be able to accomplish its inspiring task as a community. A specialization of ministries, in other words. That is a simple sociological fact and my study of the question has enabled me to recognize the legitimacy of that sociological fact both in the earliest communities of Jesus and in the present-day basic, critical communities. And that is theologically significant for me.

O. *In a number of critical communities that I know at first hand, all kinds of people have functions, even in the liturgy, and they would be very surprised if you were to call them 'office-bearers'.*

S. Of course they would. The whole of that traditional terminology has lost its meaning in the situation in which so many critical communities find themselves. But I would certainly say this: What those people are in fact doing has always been called 'office' in the Church.

O. *I simply can't imagine the people who lead in that way in the Amsterdam student* ecclesia *or in any other similar critical community letting themselves be 'ordained'.*

S. It is not really a question of ordination as we know it from the history of the Church. It is a question of the gesture or the sign in which a particular woman or man who belongs to the community is given a mandate. The Protestants do that with the laying on of hands or whatever, but it takes place in a liturgical setting. I know quite a number of pastoral workers who are working in a community and they are often accepted by that community in a liturgical gathering. That is, as far as I am concerned, ordination. The bishops don't accept it, of course, because it doesn't seem to have the same significance as classical ordination. But that is reasoning on the basis of a Church order which is no longer fruitful, but which has to be preserved at any price. And then, of course, there is inevitably conflict.

But what are you to do if a leader — a man or a woman — has emerged in a community, but if, according to canon law, that leader may not take the lead in the Eucharist or in a penitential celebration or in anointing the sick and so on? That, no more and no less, is the basis of the whole conflict with canon law. What is the solution? I would say it is first and foremost the task of theologians to show in their professional capacity that this new praxis is both theologically possible and pastorally necessary. If all theologians throughout the whole world were to say that and support it with real arguments, the hierarchy of the Church would have to change.

O. *But you are the only theologian, with your book* Ministry, *to have done this so far.*

S. The English translation of that book has reached Poland and I have had several letters from there. And priests, some of them vicars general in a diocese, have written to me from Czechoslovakia, thanking me for my book and saying: 'We have been thinking along the same lines, but were not sure whether it was theologically possible'. So they feel their thinking is justified by this theological view. I think it will penetrate in the long run and have an effect.

Many many priests have closed their account with the Church authorities. They feel that this is pastorally justified, but they are not sure whether it is theologically justified. I think my book on office in the Church — *Ministry* in English — makes a contribution to this. It can help to form attitudes and to help people with their inhibitions regarding dogma and all kinds of out-of-date theological views.

O. *Do you think your view will make it?*

S. I am convinced it will. But I am also sure the Church will not abandon its historically developed position so quickly. But even in that document published by the Holy Office on women in office in the Church — although it rejects the idea of women holding office, there is a cautious note that indicates that everything is not quite so certain. You can see at least that they are conscious of the need for change. The only thing they really defend is their present position, the existing Church order. So how will anything be changed? Well, change will come about in the Church as it always has — via the facts themselves, in other words, via the critical communities. But, when that happens, you always have conflict with the official Church. The pope won't accept it — he will, of course, want to keep to the prevailing Church order. And then, of course, all the bishops have to follow suit. But they won't be able to continue doing that for long.

O. *What does 'long' mean in this context? Fifty years?*

S. Well, it is obvious that it will go on as it is at present for some time. We are living now in what I would call a period of restoration. That doesn't just apply to the Church. The whole world is moving to the right at present. That is because of the crisis. And, of course, there are all the usual phenomena — people as a mass longing for a really strong personality in leadership and so on. The present pope, with his world tours and his very firm pronouncements, plays on that need and even non-Catholics and atheists are impressed — great numbers of them!

And then, of course, many of the renewals both in the Church and in society at large have simply taken place at the higher cultural level and haven't penetrated to the masses. There has been a great deal of progress and development, but alongside it a very conservative culture has continued to exist. It may take almost a century before the progressive culture really becomes dominant in society. There is a very lively left-wing movement that is highly critical of society and it exists all over the world. But is it typical of our present society? What is really typical of the morality of the masses of the people is, I think, the fact that 'Dallas' or something very similar can be seen everywhere on all the TV channels throughout the whole world in the evening! That is surely the dominant culture!

I think for the next ten or even fifteen years we shall see even more restoration of this kind, in the Netherlands generally and in the Church. The situation here has hardly been rose-coloured since the synod of Dutch bishops met in Rome in January 1980! On the other hand, there is every reason for hope, because we know from history that every time there is a firm attempt to impose restoration, there is an equally firm resistance. I think that the Roman determination to restore will increase the opposition of the basic communities to the establishment. That seems to me to be the only hope. At the base of the Church there are, after all, so many people who know what it's all about, people with very sound common sense who won't admit defeat to a bishop or a pope.

My own father is a typical example! He is ninety-six and has always been a thorough-going Catholic. But he has never wanted to make a 'pilgrimage' to Rome and he has never had any 'devotion' to the pope. When I had my first difficulties with Rome, it was made public, of course, and was on the television. A journalist interviewed my father and asked him: 'What do you think about this affair? You are a Catholic and now your son is under suspicion by the pope?' My father said at once: 'I know Edward, but I don't know this pope'.

O. *Those people at the base, who know what it's all about — would they, do you think, feel drawn to what Cardinal Willebrands said in the name of all the Dutch bishops in his letter dated 25 June 1982 and entitled 'Servant in God's community. The office of the priest in the Catholic Church.' In that letter, Cardinal Willebrands took up a very clear position against your views and especially against all those who, whether they have been inspired by you or not, have gone over to practices that are not permitted according to canon law. It was clear from your first reactions to this episcopal admonition that you didn't want a quarrel with the bishops. In fact the* Volkskrant *reported on 2 July, to the astonishment of many readers: 'Schillebeeckx reacts positively to the Cardinal's letter' and, according to that report, you said: 'I would have expressed some of the statements made rather differently, but on the whole I would endorse the letter'. Then you quoted the essence of your own view and insisted that the letter made no contribution 'to a solution of problems that are as large as life itself'. Willebrands, you claimed, was appealing to the 'message of the Second Vatican Council concerning the office of the priesthood' and was asking for 'understanding and empathy with regard to the text in the light of faith'. Almost as though his readers were considering the gospel itself.*

May I quote a passage from Cardinal Willebrands' letter and ask you if you would perhaps 'have expressed some of the statements rather differently', to quote your own words, at least according to the report in the Volkskrant:

'It is only when we fully accept the conciliar text in faith that it communicates its content to us at the deepest level. It then presents itself to us not only as a guide, but also as an appeal and not only as a theological norm, but also as a kerygmatic summons. Are we not perhaps influenced in our discussions and when we present our own opinions to others in a too one-sided way by sociological or psychological guide-lines that are in themselves very reasonable? I do not deny that these and other similar data must be integrated into our guidance of the Church, but they must be included within the context of the Christian experience of faith, Christian trust and the Christian view of faith' (Servant in god's community, *p.11*).

*The suggestion, then, is that you do not do that or that you do it insufficiently —
that you present your own opinions 'in a too one-sided way, being led by
guide-lines that are in themselves very reasonable . . .'*

S. Cardinal Willebrands' letter reproduces, in broad outline at least, what
Vatican II had to say about office in the Church. But in Vatican II, as in all
the other councils of the Church, faith and theology overflow into each
other. The Council made no clear distinction between faith and theology
in its documents and it is interesting to note that the official documents
have an Accompanying Letter, in which it is said quite explicitly that the
authoritative value of the different conciliar texts and the various parts
of those texts has to be interpreted 'according to the usual criteria of
interpretation' of conciliar documents.

So I have certain misgivings when the Cardinal says: 'I speak in the
light of the faith of the Church' and I would not do that myself. The
theologian's task, however, is as far as possible to make a distinction
between the aspect of faith and the purely theological aspect, even though
it is true to say that faith is always expressed as faith that has been
subjected to theological reflection. This has also to be borne in mind by the
theologian.

My greatest objection to the Cardinal's letter, however, is that he speaks
in it about living things, events and people in the Church exclusively
in the language of faith. I do the very opposite — I speak about the
event of the Church, the whole event, lock, stock and barrel (at least
everything in it that can be analysed historically, sociologically and socio-
psychologically) and include all that in the language of faith. That is, I
think, speaking in real terms in the light of faith and at the same time it
also points to the greater possibilities open to faith, certainly in structural
matters.

What the Cardinal says in the language of faith I would fully endorse,
but that doesn't make any difference to what I said in my book about
office in the Church. Let me put it very simply. I look at what people,
believers, those holding office are doing in the Church and then try to
establish the extent to which we, who are guided by the great Christian
tradition are discovering the effective presence of Christ in it. That is what
I call doing theology in the light of faith.

The Cardinal makes a contrast in his letter between 'theoretical
questions' and 'existential questions' and that is, I think, wrong. In my
view, it is precisely the existential questions that confront us with a

theoretical question, for example, as to whether a firm theory may not be an obstacle to the praxis of faith. It is precisely here, I think, that a careful distinction has to be made between faith and theology.

In fact, the difference between what the Cardinal says and what I am saying is this: I am pleading for a few changes to be made in Church order or in canon law. The Cardinal, on the other hand, is reasoning on the basis of a canon law that cannot be changed. There is no question of changing faith! But there is a need to change pastoral policy and ultimately to change . . . hierarchical control. That control is in the hands of the bishops and, of course, the pope. The theologians have no control — they only have the 'word' at their disposal.

O. *But it would seem that that 'word' does its work well. You have already said how many positive reactions there have been abroad, for example, to your book on the Church's office. I have been wondering what comment you might have to make about this: Is it not possible, do you think, that the basic groups and critical communities in the Netherlands may at a given moment decide to choose someone or at least name someone who would watch over the relationship between the groups as a whole in the name of all the others, someone, in other words, with an 'episcopal' function — a person who would work for mutual understanding between all the critical groups and encourage them to correct each other, to put critical questions to each other and to check one insight suggested by one community against another insight put forward by another group?*

S. You have put the question very acutely. If the Vatican doesn't change, that will certainly happen in the long run and it won't be the result of a decision made in an office, but will just come about in the life of the communities themselves. That is really how the episcopate developed in the Church in the second century. Until about 150 A.D. there were no bishops. The Church had a presbyterial structure. But there was a need for contacts between different local churches and this gave rise to a kind of 'administration' with a co-ordinating function and also providing leadership, at least to some extent. Of course, critical communities are very wary of this kind of development and indeed of anything that even remotely resembles a new Church order. But something of the kind will certainly happen. The communities will not want to continue in isolation, standing on their own. The first move in this direction has perhaps already been taken — the creation in Utrecht of a secretariat for the whole basic movement. In the long run, a 'bishop' will emerge from the movement or whatever they decide to call him.

10
The liberation of the poor

O. *I think it must be easier for the basic communities in the Third World, in Latin America, for example, and even for those in Italy to resist what you call 'restoration' than it is for critical communities in the Netherlands, because they have very obviously political and social tasks and because they are very closely united with each other in those tasks. When those tasks predominate, it's much easier to relativize the prevailing Church ideology, to disregard it and not to indulge in polemics about it. They are, in a sense, in a 'privileged' situation, because, as Bert ter Schegget has said, they are 'partisans', working for the interests of the poor.*

We in the Netherlands and in Europe generally are so busy with problems of Church order and we are so preoccupied with the struggle to have pastoral workers recognized, to have women admitted to office in the Church and to have obligatory celibacy removed and so on. We are frustrated by these things and ashamed that they take up so much of our time. But the great question is still this: Can the existing churches in Western Europe and North America and can the Roman Catholic Church in particular ever be an instrument for the liberation of the poor?

S. That is for me too a very great question. And I think the future of the Church is no longer to be found in Europe or North America. That is quite clear from all those synods in Rome. All those new voices that are to be heard there. During Vatican II, it was European voices that could still be heard — a few cardinals. But that is a long time ago now. All those people are encapsulated, isolated. No, the future is in Latin America and Africa. I am convinced of it.

They are in the majority, even quantitatively. Of course, they are still financially dependent and that makes them very vulnerable. But if a council were to be convoked now, it would in fact be a council of bishops from the Third World. And then it would not be long before we saw that the bishops from Europe and North America were the most conservative.

O. *How shall we ever really become partisans working for the liberation of the poor? In practice?*

S. It is, I think, precisely here that the religious orders are absent or at least defective. If you look at the history of the Church, you will find that the great religious orders were always critical movements and not only critical of the Church — they were also socially and politically critical. They functioned in fact as 'freedom movements'. Francis unleashed a great movement that was very critical of society and Dominic was critical of the Church's hierarchy of his own time, clearly aware of the fact that the way of life led by a rich feudal clergy made the proclamation of the gospel quite impotent, so he initiated an entirely new form of proclamation. The same can be said of Ignatius in the sixteenth century and the Jesuit style of proclaiming the gospel.

O. *Bert ter Schegget has made a very interesting suggestion: Critical Christians should commit themselves and each other, by taking a 'vow' of solidarity with the poor and deprived. They should commit themselves solemnly to organize their lives and to make choices in such a way that they will remain as close as possible to the poor and the socially deprived. This is in principle a formulation of a special kind of 'spirituality'. Is it possible, do you think, for that spirituality to be given form in what used to be called a religious order? Do you think, in other words, that a new religious order might come from the movement of critical communities?*

S. A religious order ought to come from the basic movement, yes. But it ought to be a modern religious order.

O. *What form could such a modern religious order take?*

S. I have thought a good deal about this question, but I don't believe it can ever simply be a matter of theory. It has to be a matter of inspired *praxis*, which will in turn call for reflection. There must, in other words, be Christians who will do it, acting in the first place on an impulse, an inspiration. Reflection will follow.

What are traditionally called the 'three vows' will, I am sure, have some part to play in a movement of this kind, which may be based on a vow of solidarity with the deprived among us. Some Christians may interpret this as implying a vow of celibacy 'in solidarity'. 'We cannot do anything else', they may say, 'because we want to be everything for those who are enslaved.' Others, on the other hand, may feel that they can only derive the same power from the security of a love-relationship that is inspired by the same need for solidarity.

All the same, I think that the decisive factor, at least at the present moment of time, will be 'solidarity in *poverty*'. If I wanted to be absolutely consistent, I would have to give up my professional way of life and adopt a completely different life-style. At present I live in a middle-class environment and so I certainly follow a middle-class way of life. And I don't think that, however critical and inspired such an environment may be, it will ever spark off a really vital movement among younger people. 'Something' may be detonated, that is true, but it won't be what will lead to the emergence of a modern religious order, a modern movement, that is, which is based on ancient inspirations.

That is why I am simply always on the look-out for initiatives that younger people themselves may be inspired to take. I may perhaps be able to give them some help in this, and that is all. I certainly cannot think out a new religious model for them. In view of my own age — I am sixty-eight, after all — I think the time has come for me, perhaps not silently, but at least just remaining in the background, to watch and see what sort of things younger people have in their minds. That is my hope, anyway.

I do sometimes feel, of course, that young people don't measure up to what we older ones have expected of them and I find that pitiful and even though I am getting older, I don't give up! In fact, I often think we older ones — I mean those of us who are more than sixty-five — have got more to tell the younger generation than the generation in the middle has, the generation that the younger ones are apparently beginning to react against now.

I haven't really answered your question, I know, but I have told you something about my own desires and expectations. Perhaps, when I begin to make use of my retirement, I shall have a chance to contribute something of myself. Who knows?

O. *Members of the critical communities are often discouraged by the thought that they are middle-class, welfare-state Christians, but that they don't feel at home in the existing structures and want to break through and reach something else. We want really to belong to the Third World! But how can we?*

How can we give form to that longing? We go on expressing our solidarity with the poor in the liturgy and in our preaching and we know it is valuable, giving form in words to our feeling, helping to fashion a new attitude in others and renewing our own consciences. It is not just working for the moment — it is making history in language. We have to express ourselves in that way, so that later generations, younger people, can have recourse to what we have felt and said. But there is an impasse at the end of it and we don't know how to break through it. Can we get no further than simply a change of attitude?

S. A change of attitude is a beginning. It begins with individuals and spreads to others. People who have every opportunity for increased welfare, but who dissociate themselves from it and choose something else. That is happening on a very big scale everywhere, especially among young people. It doesn't always lead to structural changes. In the Netherlands, the critical communities consist almost entirely of middle-class people. In Latin America — and in Italy apparently — the membership is to a great extent working-class. That is not the case at all here in the Netherlands. What is urgently required is a really decisive change in attitude. I think, if the critical communities manage to find a really firm social and economic base on which they are able to say something really relevant in connection with our particular situation here in the Netherlands, there will be a significant breakthrough.

I also think we can do much more than we are at present. We ought, for example, to make a much more thorough-going analysis of our own politico-economic situation. You were speaking a moment ago about an impasse and I can see evidence of that in our faculties of theology. We are deeply immersed in a study of Latin American liberation theology, for example, but we don't apply it to our own situation. Every time there is a discussion between Latin American liberation theologians or African theologians and ourselves, working here in Europe, they tell us: You are not doing anything. You have a flirting relationship with the theology of liberation, but you haven't anything to offer for your own situation.

I think that is the greatest problem at the moment, but I am not sure what is the right way forward. You can say, for example: The situation is very different here from what it is in Latin America. But my reply would be: But we are to blame for what is happening there. That idea ought to be taken very seriously by our own theologians.

O. *But even in critical communities you meet people who are not at all prepared to say: I am to blame for the situation there.*

S. I can't agree that it is right to feel personally guilty for the situation in the Third World or even to accept collective guilt for it. But we are bound to recognize that the structures are at fault — that the capitalist mode of production in the West is the cause of the disastrous situation there and that this calls for a radical process of learning. Every critical community has to learn, reflect and analyse and encourage that learning process in others.

O. *What you are saying, then, is that the critical community is a 'school', in which the members have to spend a long time learning a new attitude, inspiring and helping each other to change and to overcome indoctrination and discouraging facts and ideologies. Schools in which you can learn to think politically and make political choices.*

You have often spoken out as a theologian against the policy and the political decisions of the Christian Party here in the Netherlands. I don't get the impression that what you have said has done the Party very much harm up till now at least. The really urgent question that still remains, however, is whether you should not, as a theologian, say to everyone who calls himself a Christian: You should vote for the left

Surely that is the one real historical step that you could take now. If we were to have a left-wing government in the Netherlands in the near future, there wouldn't be a revolution in practical politics, perhaps, but it might lead to the change in attitude that we need so much and it might provide us with a different perspective. It would even create a new climate. You would probably encourage the growth of a new, progressive movement within which drastic and much more revolutionary changes might in the long run take place and we might move much more resolutely in the direction of solidarity with the Third World. Ought you not, as a theologian, to advise quite explicitly a move politically towards the left wing?

S. I agree with you completely. I wouldn't say, of course: You must vote for the Communist Party or the Labour Party. That is quite different. But at this moment of time it is a clear duty for Christians to vote, in the light of the gospel, for a left-wing party. I have no doubts at all about this. I simply do not see how it is possible to justify any other political choice in the light of the present world situation and at the same time in the light of the gospel. In the Latin American liberation theology, which is firmly orientated towards the Marxist criticism of society, there are constant references to Western capitalism. Marxism must of necessity also be a constant source of inspiration to us. But the situation that we have now, that of late capitalism, is totally different from the situation analysed by Marx. And all our economists are bourgeois economists! What we really need very urgently are economists who are inspired by the gospel and who will analyse our late capitalist society with the help of apparatus provided by Marxism. This could in turn be followed by the formation of a theory.

O. *What you are saying is that the Marxist analysis of society — not perhaps as we find it on paper, so to speak, but as a direction to follow, as a way here and now — may be a very relevant instrument for our present purpose. It can, in other words, really throw light on our own situation?*

S. I am quite convinced it can. That is why I have been very concerned with Marx in teaching theology in recent years. We must take the best that Marx has to offer and apply it to a renewed form of Christianity. And the best of Marx is his great feeling for humanity. That feeling for man is at the basis of all his teaching. His work originated with his experience of the factory workers in Manchester, where he witnessed personally the misery of the proletariat, the exploitation of children, the degradation. . . . That experience led him to look for the causes of that situation and his theories were developed as a result of his concern and involvement. His sensitivity to the material basis of our thinking and behaving and his insight into the structures and relationships in society — we have to include these in our own processes of thought.

O. *How can the so-called materialistic reading of the Bible function within that framework?*

S. I regard that way of reading the Bible as a perfectly legitimate critical supplement to the currently accepted form of exegesis, which has, so far at least, paid very little attention to the material situation — the social, political and economic situation, in other words — in which the biblical texts came about. Form criticism (which played an important part from about 1920 onwards in Tübingen — Dibelius and Bultmann were the chief representatives of this method) bore the situation of the community firmly in mind (this was summed up in the famous words *Sitz im Leben*), but that was above all concerned, of course, with the situation in the Church (*Sitz in der Kirche*).

The materialistic reading of the Bible goes further than this. It methodically explores the situation with the help of the Marxist analysis of society. It provides us, for example, with an insight into the relationship at the time between the economic infrastructure and the superstructure. It can certainly lead to a much deeper understanding of the text.

What I do object to fundamentally, however, is the way in which Beló, for example, deals with this method of examining the Bible. He treats it as though it is the only legitimate method! All the exegesis of the previous two thousand years is dismissed as 'bourgeois' and only the method of historical materialism, the Marxist interpretation of the Bible, can legitimately be applied to every passage in Scripture and I think that is very restrictive. Beló's Marxist analysis of the gospel of Luke, for example, strikes me as being not a Marxist interpretation of Luke, but a Lucan interpretation of Marx! He reverses the situation. He repeats what Marx said about dialectical materialism with regard to his own period of history and amplifies that with Lucan texts, with the result that ancient texts are confronted with a totally strange model. Well, that naturally enough gives rise to anachronisms.

By this I mean that the materialistic exegesis of the Bible very frequently ignores the great historical studies that have been made of the socio-economic situation at the time when the New Testament was being written and tries to reconstruct that social situation from the New Testament texts in the light of the Marxist model of the analysis of society. Without the mediation of a firmly based — even a 'materialistic' — analysis of the socio-economic situation of that period as a whole, however, it strikes me as essentially non-Marxist and certainly as unscientific to appeal to a materialistic method of biblical exegesis. The Bible itself provides us with very little direct information about the economic situation at that time, so we have to look for help elsewhere — at any studies that have been made of the economic history of the period. If we don't, the socio-economic situation in the case of a passage in the Bible will probably be 'postulated' on the basis of the model used. But it would take me too long to quote examples of how the materialistic method of interpreting the Bible has thrown a much clearer light on certain biblical texts and other examples of how a specific interpretation is forced on texts by the *a priori* method (with its implicit philosophy).

O. *There is one question that is always arising. Is the materialistic method of interpreting Scripture — are Christians who are socialists perhaps not too socially and politically orientated in their understanding of liberation? Should they not be more concerned with the witness borne by the New Testament, which may point to a liberation that takes place above all inwardly? Is salvation, in other words, proclaimed in the gospel as personal salvation or as social salvation?*

S. That was, of course, the basis of the debate between Marx and Feuerbach. Marx insisted that it had to take place through the social and economic structures. Feuerbach believed it had to be a personal and inner conversion. Now many people are saying: The Marxist vision is reflected in the Old Testament, where liberation is a social and political event, but the New Testament stresses *metanoia* — a change of heart. But that is, of course, only one part of what we call Judaeo-Christian revelation. The New Testament does in fact place the emphasis on interiority. You have to take it as it is. But at the same time, it is clearly stated: The kingdom of God is at hand, so be converted (*metanoeite*). In other words, a change of attitude is called for, so that the kingdom of God can become a reality as justice among men.

But how can you change if structures that are not free and that enslave you have become part of your own inner being? There is obviously an interplay between structural change and a change of heart. You can, of course, say, as Paul did and the younger Sartre: I can be free even though I am in prison. (The Stoics said that too.) But that was said because it seemed to be impossible to change the structures. Freedom consisted of ignoring the structures, trying to rise above them and saying: I am inwardly free. An affirmation of the free 'I' as opposed to the structures of society. That was a kind of partial freedom, of course.

The peace proclaimed by Jesus, however, is universal peace and the freedom he proclaims is also universal — shalom. His movement found its recruits among the poor and the enslaved (and there were also intellectuals among them who financed the communities). What could those people do, given the political system of that period? Practically nothing. What they were able to do is stressed again and again in the synoptics. It was: 'You know how things are in the world — how those in power rule with rod of iron. That must not happen among you.'

In the Christian community, then, a change of heart always goes together with a change in the structure of community life. There can be no master-slave relationships in the community, which is one of sisters and brothers. The community of believers is a model for what ought to happen later in the world. In the Bible, personal conversion and working for a new social structure go together. Then, later, as circumstances change, this interrelationship led to — or should have led to — Christian communities being committed to political change as a consequence of the gospel, as something that is completely in accordance with the gospel! Change can never, in Christianity, be simply and exclusively inner change.

That contrast between the inner life and the outside world has, moreover, been superseded. There is no need to make such a clear distinction between the two. To do so is to set up a new kind of dualism. Norbert Elias has shown that very convincingly in his book *Über den Prozess der Zivilisation*. He has established beyond doubt that our inner life is completely filled with the society around us and, because of this, often 'alienated'.

O. *But what is that* metanoia *preached by Jesus? Theologians have called it* sola gratia — *only grace. Don't we have that conversion within our own power, then? Can't we bring it about ourselves? How are we to proclaim that* metanoia, *that inner conversion?*

S. I suppose you could say that, if everyone in the world experienced that inner conversion, the structures of society would change of their own accord. But that is, of course, obviously a utopian solution. So, because of the dialectical tension that exists between our personal inner life and the world outside, between individual and social structures, you have to begin with both at the same time.

O. *But what is inner conversion?*

S. You are converted inwardly when you choose in favour of solidarity with others. That is quite clear from the gospel — you are called on to liberate others, to set others free first. That is why I am so critical of this leaning towards the East. It is always a question of one's own freedom in Eastern mysticism. In our present circumstances, however, it must above all be a question of the freedom of our fellow-men. That was certainly so in the case of Jesus. He didn't fight for his own freedom. He always fought for other people's freedom.

O. *What is 'at hand' in the words 'the kingdom of God is at hand'?*

S. Justice among men as a gift of God.

O. *But in what sense are we to understand that? After all, the injustice of the social system in which we are living, the injustice of what we used to call our capitalist mode of production, is becoming increasingly obvious. At the same time, people — individuals — are becoming increasingly aware that they can only participate fully in a process of change to the extent that they have themselves become inwardly changed and more completely at one with others. . . . So I suppose you could say that is what is at hand, what is approaching. Or am I expressing it in too horizontal a way?*

S. No, I don't think so. In Matthew 6, for example, we read: 'Seek first his kingdom *and* his righteousness'. God's justice is a gift, but we have to make it a reality in the power of that grace.

O. *But how is it a gift? How does it break through as a gift?*

S. That is the old dispute between the Jesuits and the Dominicans, isn't it? Grace and freedom — two realities, dialectically opposed, that have to be reconciled with each other. I think it is really a pseudo-problem. As soon as you believe in God as the ground and source, as the Lord of history, then you are able to see what men are doing in freedom, their free social actions, as grace. But it's a false problem, because you can't contrast that *sola gratia* with freedom. On the other hand, you can't speak about the fact that free human commitment is itself grace in a single language game.

So we have to say, for example, it is a freedom movement, as in Latin America, which can be sociologically analysed so that the causes can be discovered. But if there is a question of the genuine liberation of men and women in that movement, then I would say: *sola gratia*. That whole liberation movement as a movement of social, economic and political freedom is grace: *sola gratia*.

Some writers — even Gutiérrez in his earliest books — say: That liberation movement is, of course, good human activity and then you have to add something else: 'grace', the inner forgiveness of sin and so on. I think that is a form of dualism. No, it is that movement of liberation itself, political liberation from the power of the ruling class in other words, that is grace.

O. *It is possible, for example, to say this: In that social, economic and political struggle for liberation, not only in Latin America, but also here in Europe and America, in people who are trying to change their attitude and to achieve solidarity with the poor and oppressed, there is a power that is present and active in us, created in us, that makes us move in the direction of freedom?*

S. That is going to be the theme of my next great book. I haven't decided on the title yet, but I am quite sure what the contents will be. Putting it in rather theological, technical language, it will deal with a theory of God's Spirit in terms of an ecclesiology and I shall try in it to provide an insight into the blowing of God's Spirit in what messianic communities are and in what they are saying and doing. Faith in creation plays a very important part in this. If you believe in God, the creator of heaven and earth, then that creation is itself the beginning of the whole process of liberation. Wherever people are trying to bring about a way of life that is more worthy of man in history, there is salvation, grace.

O. *That is, you would say, God-in-people?*

S. Yes, that is God-in-people.

O. *That is Holy Spirit?*

S. Yes, that is the Spirit active in history. Even Vatican II said that the Spirit is active in the great social movements that are taking place in the world. And the more I think about it, the more convinced I become that we have for far too long thought about salvation too much as something that takes place within the Church. God achieves salvation in history and he does it through people. He never does it outside people. That salvation is, of course, expressed and celebrated as a theme in the Church. Faith in God for me is believing in God's universal will to save all men. Faith in God is the foundation of my hope for a better and more human world. If that faith is affirmed, then it means salvation is achieved in history and in God's name by men and women. History is never neutral. It is always a history of salvation or the absence of salvation. A freedom movement such as the one in Nicaragua is not neutral. It is also neither salvation nor the absence of salvation.

O. *What is it, then?*

S. If it succeeds in setting men free — as it seems to be doing in Nicaragua — then it is grace, salvation, that is taking place there.

O. *That power that is active in people, making them move in the direction of liberation — would you call it God-in-people? Are they synonymous?*

S. Salvation is certainly achieved by those movements. They undoubtedly bring either physical or social wholeness. But salvation from God is universal. Emancipative self-liberation is salvation for human beings. As a Christian, I would call that redemption. Christian salvation in its totality, however, is more than that, however much it may also be that as well.

The real question is: How do we go beyond that in a post-revolutionary situation? If it turns out to be no more than a mere change, an exchange of power, then, of course, we are bound in the name of the gospel to protest against it.

11

The foundation of hope

O. *God as creator, as the ground and source. You say that is going to be one of the themes of your third great book. Can you explain what you mean by 'ground and source'?*

S. I mean that, in the freedom of his actions, man draws strength from God's absolute freedom, which is pure positivity. By freedom of action, I mean action that is set free from social alienations and is therefore a freedom for good. Freedom for evil or for injustice, on the other hand, is opposition to the ground and source of all freedom in its arbitrary independence and therefore is no less than an absence of freedom. Man's impulse for good and God's grace cannot be added together!

O. *Would you say that impulse to freedom is created in us?*

S. You have used that phrase already: created in us. I don't know whether it ought to be used in this context. It is really a historically highly charged term. What I am trying to say is that man is created, that God is the creator and that the whole of creation is permeated with God's saving intention. That intention has to be made into a reality by men. Man is not just confronted with a God who is a creator — he is also confronted with a God of salvation. This is really quite important from the theological and conceptual point of view. Man's own power to act has to be defined in himself as autonomy and that same autonomy has then to be interpreted as grace. In that case, the concept of creation is not sufficient. That is why I say that the God of Israel, the liberator God (the God of salvation) is the creator. This does away with the entire conceptual difficulty between salvation and creation. Creation is the point of departure for the whole of the covenant and the whole of the movement of liberation in which universal salvation is to be achieved for all mankind.

O. *Would you say God as the ground and source is a formula of faith?*

S. It is for me the articulation, the expression of what is faith in creation.

O. *How do you come to the point where you have that faith? What form does it take in you?*

S. It is quite a complicated process, in which both experiences of the world (experiences such as finiteness) and contacts with the Christian tradition act as mediators. Faith must be firmly implanted in man. It must have a horizontal context in our humanity in this world, in which we encounter the datum of religions. There should be no hiatus between what comes from the depths of human inspiration and from human impulses and what is experienced as grace.

Karl Barth gives the impression, as do several Catholic theologians, that 'grace' comes down to us vertically from heaven without any historical or human mediation. God then only comes into view in those situations in which we are defective and can no longer continue on our own — in other words, when we have to appeal to something or someone who transcends us. But I do not look for God only in extreme situations, in which people are impotent and fall silent — when there is suffering and death. No, I also look for him in ordinary, everyday life, in situations in which people are looking for meaning in the midst of non-sense and are hoping to find justice, happiness and greater humanity. It is within that context that I want to look for what 'God' may mean.

Believing in God is speaking about the absolute that is at stake in the relative, that is, in the historical praxis of men, often as a matter of life and death. That absolute character of faith in God is revealed in what is particular, historical and relative — in this or in that particular praxis, for example, the praxis of giving a glass of water to a man who is thirsty. Whoever wants to experience the absolute in a pure form, divorced from particular and relative praxis, will never be confronted with it. It is in the important and the insignificant things of everyday experience that we have to discover how man's affair is God's affair and how God's affair must become man's affair. Speaking about God as salvation or as a liberator therefore always takes place in a 'second language game'. We speak, in other words, in the language of faith about something that has already been expressed in our profane experience. Freedom and grace are therefore to be found in one and the same reality — our human activity. The same thing is therefore said in a universally human language game, a descriptive or an analytical language game or in the language game of faith, taking faith in God the creator as our point of departure.

The question inevitably arises, of course, and you have already asked it: How do you come to the point where you have that faith in God the creator? Do you have that faith on the authority of the Word of God, the Bible, the tradition of the Church, synods, councils or the pope? In the past, that faith was accepted as a matter of course and uncritically by everyone. Everyone believed and so your own faith was confirmed and supported by the society in which you lived. In modern, pluralistic society, that social consent has disappeared and this, of course, undermines many people's faith. So the Christian has, in the circumstances that prevail nowadays, to justify why he or she believes in God. The Christian should not, of course, have a heavier burden to carry here than the man or woman who does not believe in God! But he or she must be able to throw light on the meaning of his or her faith and be able to show as clearly as possible what is meant when he or she speaks about God.

Let me illustrate what I mean by this, at least in broad outline. The believer must be able to show (a) that there are universally shared experiences which all people inevitably share in common with each other (for example, experiences of finiteness and contingency), experiences which concern the totality of our human existence at the deepest level and which therefore give rise to emotional reactions; (b) experiences which, on the one hand, should not be interpreted apodictically, that is, with convincing rational force, in the direction of faith in God, but (c) which, on the other hand, are, in their total experiential content, of the kind that they can be more meaningfully clarified by faith in God than by remaining silent about God. This does not result in an attempt to prove the existence of God, but it does mean that you can make it clear that the universally human phenomenon 'religions' or 'communities of believers' is meaningfully implanted in universally human experiences.

Every experience (even the experience of a non-believer) is always an interpreted experience and that applies also to the experience of human finiteness or, to express it in a different way, the experience of an absolute frontier. Sartre analysed that experience very precisely. And non-believers are bound to admit that that experience is not a projection made by men, but a given reality of our humanity. What non-believers experience interpretatively, however, as the 'last word' ('we have been thrown on our own into an alien world'), the believer will experience interpretatively as the mediation (for us) of the absolute saving presence of God: 'having been thrown' has nonetheless been a 'being held' by God's hand. This faith does not in any way take away the risk of human adventure, but the believer knows that his name has been written in the palm of God's hand. Of course, that is an act of faith, I know that, but it is not made in the dark. You can, as a believer, throw light on the meaningful and rational nature of that self-giving in faith without resorting to evident rationality. Is convincing rationality the supreme attribute of man, the mystery?

O. *So for you the experience of man's finite and limited nature is an experience of God?*

S. That is one of the approaches in which I am conscious of the saving presence of God in human life and history and that the content of my faith is mediated by human experience. If that mediation is not there, I cannot see on what basis it can be accepted.

O. *Is it not possible for someone to interpret his own human experience of completeness and unlimited possibility as the image and likeness of God? You appear to reject that emphatically.*

S. Yes, I reject that. That unlimited factor may be infinite and vague, especially in its aim — a random shot in the dark. Then there is no eschaton, no completion, no fulfilment, a history leading nowhere.

O. *I was really thinking of the experience that people are capable of having of love, the fact that, despite their limitations and shortcomings and despite all the suffering they cause to each other, they can be good to each other and are capable of loving. That is surely an absolute experience.*

S. I don't think the two should ever be separated. In fact I am sure that if you were to speak simply about absolute frontiers or limits, you would not get very far. But it seems to me to be a fundamental datum as a point of departure at least. That is because experience of a frontier — an absolute frontier — always implies the question: Can we go beyond that frontier? Even Albert Camus was conscious of the need for love to spread out into our environment, both on a small and on a large scale, but in his experience love was absolutely limited and not capable of revealing a perspective in the direction of God. I would prefer to take our experience of positive love among our fellow-men and absolute limitation together as a single, undivided phenomenon that calls for clarification. There is, in my opinion, a meaningful perspective pointing in the direction of God in that experience.

O. *The poor and deprived members of our society, you said earlier on, are the ones who pronounce eschatological judgement. Levinas has spoken about the face of my fellow-man, my neighbour in need, looking at me and asking for recognition. That face judges me, he has said. If I am able to respond to the glance of my fellow-man, is that not an absolute experience? Surely it is an absolute experience that one man can be, as Brecht has said, another man's neighbour? Even beyond all frontiers?*

S. I see it in this way: Within the experience of our absolute limitation, the phenomenon of what Levinas calls the 'other's face', the human ethos, in other words, presents itself. Yes, I would agree with that. But ultimately, the transcendence of the 'other person' always leads to an aporia or a fundamental difficulty. That other person is for me, as I am for him, not only the origin of an ethical appeal, but also very frequently the source of threat and possible violence. Sartre pointed that out. If, within the stream of human history, man is only a source of value and meaning for his fellow-man, that is good, but we have no guarantee that what is good and right rather than what is evil and wrong will be triumphant and will have the last word to say about our existence as ethically responsible beings. According to Levinas, what cannot be traced back to inter-human relationship is a primitive form of religiosity.

What I would criticize here is the term 'trace back to' or 'reduce to'. I think religion or faith that is not incorporated into an interpersonal relationship is certainly primitive. But man's relationship with God cannot simply be traced back to interpersonal relationships. So, for me at least, both liturgical celebration and political and social commitment to one's fellow-men are extremely important and meaningful, in the human sense as well.

Martyrdom is, I think, the existential context within which it can be seen most clearly why believers are aware of a meta-ethical, in other words, a religious dimension in ethics. Think, for example, of the situation of a soldier who is confronted with the task of killing an innocent man. He refuses to so this. Yet he knows that his refusal to carry out his duty as a soldier will not prevent that innocent person from being shot and killed later by someone else and he also knows he will also lose his own life by refusing. The ethical gesture of that soldier is therefore ineffective. (The innocent person is still shot and killed.) In addition to this, the soldier also loses his own life together with all his own unrealized possibilities.

It is therefore a gesture that is both absurd and heroic. But the conclusion is that he is himself the victim of an evil empirical reality. Where, then, does the soldier get his conviction, based on faith, that right will ultimately triumph over wrong? Hoping in 'good luck', hoping against hope that right will prevail and not wrong — there is courage in that, certainly, and the soldier's ethical greatness is to be found in that courage. But what is the ground of that hope? Will right prevail if the ground of it is only to be found in man? In man with all his ambiguity?

The believer does the same as the soldier whom I have chosen as my example here, but he entrusts the absurd gratuity of that gesture to God as the source of pure positivity without any ambiguity. And that faith is itself mediated by the human conviction that right should prevail above all wrong. The person who believes in God, then, sees in the fact that right must prevail an experience of what is above humanity, an experience of transcendence, in other words, he experiences the absolute and saving presence of God in that confusion of meaning and non-sense that we call 'human existence'.

O. *We are moving on very quickly, so I must first ask you a very obvious question about God as the source of pure positivity and the absolute and saving presence of God, two formulae that you have used, and what is in stark contrast with this, the suffering and misery that men inflict on each other, their crimes against each other, their oppression of each other. . . .*

S. When you put it that way, I find myself confronted with an impenetrable wall. All that I can say is: that is not what God wants. He also does not permit it! Some theologians speak about 'God's permissive will', but that is a way of avoiding the need to state that evil is simply a mystery. Other theologians, I know, say: If you were able to see through God's plan, you would be able to accept it; it would simply be because we are ignorant that we are unable to accept suffering and evil. Well, that is, as far as I am concerned, nonsense. It also diminishes man's stature! It is just not possible to speak meaningfully about Auschwitz and, however hard you try, you can't situate it anywhere in God's plan. If it were true that God needed Auschwitz in his divine plan for man, in order to teach us a lesson or something, then I could simply no longer believe in God! It would be unthinkable.

On the other hand, you can't claim that God is defeated or that his existence is disproved by the fact of Auschwitz. After all, people who were in that concentration camp said: 'Blessed is your name!' Jews practised the kiddush in Auschwitz! God's name was blessed in those absurd circumstances in which it was impossible for people to say a meaningful word!

Since Auschwitz, of course, we have often asked where God was at that time, but our Jewish friends tell us: That is a wrong question to ask; it is God who asks us: Adam, where are you? He asks man: What have you done with your history? Well, what have we done with our history?

O. *The suffering of innocent people, you say, confronts you with an impenetrable wall.*

S. That is true. I cannot explain suffering and especially innocent suffering. Man is a creature. He is created by God. What does that mean? It means that all the good that is in man has its ultimate source, as man's goodness, in God. But that cannot be said of evil. What is negative is not created. You cannot relate negativity to God.

God wanted finite, mortal man to be. So man can only be man in a world that is 'only' world and that involves suffering. I can situate a certain amount of suffering. But there is such an excess of suffering and evil that I cannot situate it all.

Is God responsible for it? Because he wanted that free, finite man to exist in a natural world in which there were also natural disasters? Did he foresee that and still create man? Or should we say: He has accepted the consequences of human freedom?

All that I would venture to say at the moment is that God is not absent, even in the greatest suffering. He is silently present in it and that enables man to say: 'Into your hands I commit my spirit', although he doesn't know what that implies. Jesus did not die, after all, in the certain knowledge that he would rise again after his suffering and death. He was not able to situate suffering either.

O. *How do you pray, then, when you are confronted with suffering?*

S. I am despairing. Sometimes I simply swear. I swore when I heard that Oscar Romero had been murdered in San Salvador. I was angry. But then I thought: well, that is also a form of prayer, so long as it doesn't remain just swearing.

O. *How should it continue, then?*

S. It shouldn't continue with your saying: God must have an intention here, but rather with your saying: we are still in God's hands, even in grim situations like this one. This terrible event isn't the last word. And you have to say that with all the strength that is in your being.

O. *In his book on sin, Herman Wiersinga says that 'sin' is submitting passively to the facts, giving up, not confronting the future.*

S. Thomas Aquinas called despair the worst sin, *the* sin. So Wiersinga is right — sinning is giving up and not facing the future.

O. *But there are people who are by nature or for some other reason more depressive and more despairing than others. But perhaps you are not thinking of that kind of 'despair'.*

S. No, I am not. I am thinking of the kind of despair that insists: There is no salvation. I cannot be saved in this situation. This is the end. There is no future . . . *The* sin is, I think, not giving credit to God any more.

O. *So, even with regard to Auschwitz and indeed to all suffering, the ultimate ground of your hope is that God is always the source of new possibilities or because God is new every day, as you said before.*

S. Yes, my hope is based on my faith that God is pure positivity. He is the promoter of all that is good and he opposes all that is evil. He is not a God of life and death, as he would appear to be at certain levels in the Old Testament. If he were, he would be an ambiguous God. No, he is pure positivity. He fights against the beast Leviathan. He opposes evil.

Everywhere where people promote what is good and human, moreover, and combat evil, whether they are believers or not, they are affirming God's being. In their praxis, that is, in making the world a more human place to live in, they are confirming that God is love. That is for me the most convincing proof of God's existence — the praxis of good and the fight against every kind of evil.

O. *So you don't believe it is possible to prove the existence of God on the basis of personal meaningful experiences?*

S. No, they do not provide sufficient evidence in my opinion. History is full of meaning and non-sense. On what basis do you expect right to prevail? Both Kant and later Erich Bloch expressed that as a purely 'postulated' hope — you simply demand it for yourself and for reasons of self-preservation. It cannot be any different and people believe in it. If a city is destroyed by bombing during a war, people just begin all over again, rebuilding. Hope breaks through again and again.

But what is the foundation of that hope? There is surely something in man that gives him a basic hope and trust that good rather than evil will and must prevail. But how can that be justified? What is the most meaningful explanation of the existence of that hope? Is it human nature? That is a postulate, after all — we act as though history were ultimately meaningful and in fact we demand it because we oppose evil, but we really do not know. I try to justify why that hope is firmly based, for example. I cannot find any purely agnostic basis for that hope. If you look at human history, it is not difficult to find a great deal of evidence on the basis of which you can say: people want to make it as good as possible and on the basis of which you can therefore cherish hopeful expectations.

And then, despite all those expectations, you are confronted in the twentieth century with Auschwitz. You are confronted with the fact that evil strikes again and again and destroys good. That certainly seems to be what happens in history. In the end, good will prevail in history, yet I see history as ambivalent. In the light of my faith in God the creator, however, I would say: God wants it to be a history in which good will ultimately triumph and evil will be defeated. God does not want a history consisting of a confusion of sense and non-sense. He wants pure sense, pure meaning, to be ultimately achieved and by men. That knowledge, based on faith, is, I think, the ultimate and the most powerful driving force enabling men to work for a better world.

This doesn't mean that an unbelieving view is meaningless. I think it is quite heroic that people should declare: we don't know whether history will in the end be meaningful, but we must go on trying to make something meaningful of it. To live in that way as an atheist, yes, it is a very meaningful way of life. But at the same time I think that a much more powerful impulse can come from the Judaeo-Christian religion, in which God is seen as pure positivity, because our hope and our expectations are well founded, even though they may be founded on an inexpressible mystery.

O. *That mystery of God as pure positivity takes place, you think, in human history. It is brought about by people. God as pure positivity, then, 'appears' in people who do good.*

S. Yes, appears in the goodness of men and women. If I were never to see that goodness of men and women, I would not believe in God.

O. *That faith has a history in you, in me, in men and women. It has a history that can be described. You are born. You grow in a language and in a praxis that corresponds to that language. It can all be described, yet there is something in that history that cannot be described. You cannot always have a conspectus of the whole of your own history. People forget. But they also encounter themselves at a given moment as believers, perhaps in a given Church, perhaps outside the Church, and then they say: I believe. Would you say that is an experience of being chosen, of receiving grace?*

S. Yes, I would say that my experience of faith is one of grace. But I reject the idea of being chosen and I reject all forms of 'election theology'. God has chosen all men. Not just Jews or Christians. There is a creator who wants human history to be a history of salvation for all men. That is a view in which no one is discriminated against. That universal salvation, however, is 'mediated'. It comes about in and through particular events and in and through a particular history — that of the Jewish people or through that particular man Jesus of Nazareth. That is, of course, a stumbling-block for many people. It scandalizes them. But how could it ever have been any different?

In Judaeo-Christian history, you can see how slowly salvation became universal. It began with salvation for separate clans. Then it became the salvation of twelve clans and then that of a people, a nation. Then gradually the idea developed that that nation had to be at the service of the whole of mankind — Zion administering to the whole of the world. So there was a very slow growth, then, of the insight into the universal nature of God's salvation through particular events. Once again I would ask: How could it ever have been any different? That is just the way it happened.

I believe, then, that God chose the people of Israel, but that he chose them to serve the whole of mankind. The Israelites also gradually came to recognize that they had been chosen to serve the whole of mankind. They came to see that God might just as well have chosen the Philistines. The entire ideology that kept emerging in Israel with regard to their own election as the chosen people of God was again and again unmasked by the prophets, in other words, by Israelites themselves. No, election without a universal ministry — I think that is atrocious!

12

Eastern and Western spirituality

O. *When you were fifteen, you became fascinated by the Eastern religions —
Hinduism and Buddhism. In the early nineteen-seventies, tens of thousands of
Western Europeans, including very many young people looked for salvation in
those Eastern religions. Can you understand that phenomenon?*

S. Obviously many people in the West are suffering from what has been
called a 'crisis of identity'. They are not at peace with the norms and
values that are forced on them in their own society. The identity that they
are persuaded to accept they see as a false one and they are looking for a
new one. They are looking for something more — a deeper meaning in
their life. In the past, that meaning was provided by Christianity. The need
was satisfied within the framework of the Judaeo-Christian tradition, the
traditional Christian churches. But the Western religious tradition is no
longer recongizable and it no longer provides a meaningful perspective.
So many people have turned to the Eastern religious traditions. The
remarkable thing is that the opposite is also occurring. There are people in
the East who no longer accept their own cultural heritage unquestioningly and they go to America, for example, to learn about the Judaeo-
Christian tradition — Hindus and Buddhists. This kind of emigration from
one's own culture seems to be quite a common phenomenon now, but it
has always happened in history.

O. *People are not at ease in their own Western society and religious institutions
and that is impelling them to look to the East?*

S. Since the seventeenth and eighteenth centuries — since the rise of
trade capitalism and then since the emergence of industrial and monopoly

capitalism, our Western society has been motivated by profit and con-sumption, ruthless competition and achievement and my freedom at the expense of your freedom. It has been a society in which the structures almost force you to push your neighbour out of the way if you are to survive. It is a society in which the state has the task of legislating in order to create some harmony between the selfishness of its many members so that the environment is to some extent at least human. Modern bourgeois society is not just to be found in the structures — it has penetrated into our hearts, with the result that whole areas of human life and experience have been impoverished and many human possibilities have ceased to exist.

I would say that our very ability to experience has been diminished by the fact that the only part of our being that is nourished, developed and required by society is the active part. There are certain things — things that are there to be seen — which we simply no longer see. We are just incapable of seeing them because we have learned to see only from the point of view of utility. This is bound in the long run to have serious repercussions. Yes, our field of vision has been made narrower by the technocratic culture of which we have become a part.

But to return to Eastern spirituality. It is obvious that our search for that contains a very strong dose of social criticism. We are critical of our Western society, but — and this is an important aspect of our turning to the East — it is a criticism that leaves our society as it is and looks for salvation in the inner life.

Young people were in a state of revolt in the nineteen-sixties, but they soon came to realize that social structures in the West were much tougher than they had imagined. Many of them admitted defeat and submitted to the prevailing system. They no longer believed this world was even capable of being changed and improved. Others began to think of them-selves as individuals: Let us begin with ourselves, be converted in our hearts, renew our inner lives by meditation and sink down in meditation into the depths of our own being.

O. *Would you say that was the distinctive aspect of Eastern spirituality — sinking down in meditation into the depths of one's own being? What takes place when you do that?*

S. Our own being becomes, as it were, obscured in a process of self-dispossession and it tries in this way to gain access to an infinite space, and unknown sphere, a completely different, but very near world, in which everything is reconciled with everything and everyone else and the antitheses that are experienced so painfully in everyday life are removed.

O. *Does that mystical experience not belong to the heritage of the Christian tradition as well? That process of self-dispossession, self-emptying, that way of not knowing — surely those have been described by John of the Cross, for example, and Master Eckhart? Would all those Westerners who have made a physical or spiritual pilgrimage to the East not be able to find what they are seeking in the West? It would seem not!*

S. The simple fact seems to be that the Western religious tradition does not function for many Westerners. I think, however, that it is quite important to point out in this context that, although there are fundamental and sometimes even literal similarities between Eckhardt, for example, and Indian mysticism, there are also great differences — and I would think even fundamental differences.

To illustrate what I mean by this, let me briefly outline some of the most important aspects of authentically Eastern and authentically Western spirituality. Both forms of spirituality were originated, it should be noted, in the same continent — Asia. We ought therefore to speak of two Asiatic forms of religiosity: the form that began in Eastern Asia, that is, Hinduism, Buddhism and Jainism, with Zen-Taoism perhaps, and the Western Asiatic type: Judaism, Christianity and Islam.

The religions of Eastern Asia are primarily religions of the inner life, even though they all have a very complex form of external ritual. There is no confrontation between man and the divine element, which is experienced as the ground of man's innermost self and at the same time the ground of the entire cosmos, in which plurality is experienced as unity. The divine is also regarded as impersonal or rather as suprapersonal, as a mystery of compassion embracing everything. The human personality is not intensified to the level of self-consciousness by the divine element, nor is it emphasized in any way. Even human history and commitment to work for a better world — aspects of life that are so stressed here in the West — have a purely relative value in the religions of the East. The prototype of these religions is, I think, the yogi, sitting in the lotus position, silent, passive, turned inwards on himself and away from the world and at one with the power that reconciles everything with itself.

The religions of Western Asia are sharply contrasted with those of the East. Judaism, Christianity and Islam are all, I think, characterized by their emphasis on a personal God who speaks to man, questions him and challenges him. This confrontation that takes place between God and man in the West is done through prophets — these Western religions are above all prophetic religions. God makes man, who is created in his image, responsible for history. Man becomes himself in a historical confrontation with his God. He becomes an individual person who is free and who has the right to speak and even to speak with God. The classical example of this is, of course, the Old Testament figure of Job. All three religions — Judaism, Christianity and Islam — are therefore directed firmly towards ethical action, in other words, Jews, Christians and Muslims all have the task of establishing the kingdom of God as a kingdom of justice among men.

O. *Is there no room in those religions, then, for mysticism — for a mystical unity between man and the divine element, as you call it? Is that, in your opinion, the fundamental difference between the Western and the Eastern Asiatic religions?*

S. The inspiration of the Western religions, with their marked orientation towards the world, is a very central mystical experience. Moses was a political leader and the liberator of his people, but he was at the same time also a mystic who spoke 'face to face' with God, 'as a man speaks to his friend'. Mohammed had encounters in the depths of night with Allah's angels, who, as it were, communicated God's word, the Quran, to him directly from heaven. Jesus also had a mystical experience of God as his Father and that was the source of the whole of his life in service of the poor and the enslaved people of this world.

O. *So there is reference both in Hinduism and Buddhism on the one hand and in the Islamic and the Judaeo-Christian tradition on the other to mystical experience. But there is, surely, a great difference in the way in which that experience functions, in the way in which it works in each of the two branches of Asiatic religion? In Christianity, you would say, mysticism points in a direction that is different from that of the 'Eastern religions', to give them that name just for the sake of convenience.*

S. It would be an inner contradiction to speak of religion without mysticism. There is clearly mysticism in both types of religion. Yes, the difference is certainly to be found in the way in which that mysticism, which is present in both, functions.

The mystical tendency is present in the Eastern religions — it is quite a convenient name — without any connection at all with the socio-political order. What is more important even, that mystical tendency was — and, moreover, can without difficulty be historically proved to have been — brought into existence in order to justify the caste-system in India. The whole doctrine of reincarnation, which plays such an important part in the Eastern religions, is a justification of that caste-system. Only the members of the highest caste can break out of that structure and, by becoming poor, express their solidarity with the poorest members of society! The poor themselves and the members of the lowest caste cannot break out! They have to observe the rules of their own caste (dharma) until the end of their lives and can only hope to rise to the next level, a higher caste, in a second life. Surely that is a pure justification of a very chaotic society! I think everyone who is attracted to Eastern religiosity ought to take that fact very much into account!

There are many aspects of Western Christian mysticism which are very similar to aspects of Hindu mysticism, but it is impossible to establish a direct influence between the two. It is worth noting, however, that Master Eckhardt has pointed out that the model of all mysticism is not the contemplative Mary, but the active Martha! In other words, according to Eckhardt, mysticism which does not result in improving society is a false mysticism. What is more, the great powers in Western society always misuse every mystical revival. In America, for example, many centres of meditation are financed from the top. That is not because of a desire to subsidize praiseworthy cultural phenomena. It is the result of a cool, calculating look at those phenomena — the more young people withdraw from society into contemplation, the more the revolutionary potential is reduced and made impotent. It's an effective way of silencing criticism of the prevailing social structures! Encourage people who reflect to meditate, isolate them and let them stay on the periphery of society! Then our contemporary society, which is based on achievement and which aims to keep the poor poor, will not be disturbed by criticism.

O. *Will there, do you think, be no place in a renewed Christian tradition for professional contemplatives in monasteries or in some other form of community?*

S. Yes, I think there should always be specialization of a traditional kind, on the one hand, a special form of prophetism and, on the other, mysticism. In Christianity, there has always been a tradition of the active religious whose function was prophetic and critical and a parallel tradition of contemplative monks, who were orientated above all towards mysticism. If there were no medical specialists, there would be no general concern in society for physical health. Specialists are necessary to remind and admonish everyone constantly. Yes, I think there ought to be centres both of prophecy and of mysticism in the future.

O. *I think I would be interpreting your way of thinking correctly if I were to say that you would like to see the most powerful and the most distinctive tendencies within both Eastern and Western spirituality growing together to form a new religious culture. Do you notice any signs of this growth already?*

S. So far I have not seen any real sign of a higher synthesis between Christianity and Eastern religiosity, although there are, I believe, Buddhist Christians. There are also typically Indian Christologies, but I am not sure whether they are faithful both to Eastern spirituality and to the distinctive nature of Christianity. The Indian theologian Pannikar has almost completely eliminated the historical Jesus, with whom he does not know what to do, but he has been able to 'translate' the risen Christ, the principle of Christ, you might say, into Eastern mystical terms.

It is also only really possible to understand another tradition fully, I think, when your own tradition and the other one come together in a shared experience. That happened in the West when the Jewish and the Greek traditions came together. It is possible for Western Christians, then, to understand Judaean and Greek thought.

O. *For them to understand? Still, do you think? They used to understand those two traditions, at least to some extent. We were talking earlier on about the Jewish-Hellenistic formula of faith in our creed: Jesus as 'one in being with the Father'. I have the impression that Jewish and Greek thought are still in conflict with each other, in what might be called 'linguistic conflict'. But when you analysed that phrase 'one in being', you showed how that linguistic conflict could be overcome and you insist now that the two traditions, the Jewish and the Greek, have merged together to become a single tradition. There has been a shared experience: unique and definitive salvation has been given in the historical Jesus of Nazareth both for the Jews and for the Greeks and the division between them has been healed in Jesus. And in the same way, you are claiming, if I interpret you correctly, there can be a synthesis between Christianity and Eastern religiosity as a result of the shared experience that definitive and complete salvation has been given in the historical Jesus both for the East and for the West, 'to the ends of the earth'.*

S. Yes, I think that synthesis will be possible in the distant future. But the process by which it is reached is much more difficult than many people think. The dialogue between Western and Eastern spirituality is still in its infancy. The synthesis between Judaism and Hellenism took centuries, after all! Eastern techniques of meditation have been enjoying a certain popularity for some time now in the West. Most of us in the West are so active that we have lost our sense of equilibrium and are permanently out of breath. We can't even do our ordinary day-to-day tasks peacefully. Yes, we should learn how to breathe properly! We would be fitter if we did. We must learn correct breathing before learning specific methods of religious experience that are distinctively Eastern in tradition. Then we may become eventually as inspired as the Hindus and Buddhists can be as a result of living in that religious environment. . . .

O. *Would you not say that the essential question that is answered differently in the East and in the West is: religion as a flight from the world or religion as turning towards the world?*

S. That dilemma does not strike me as absolute and insurmountable. There is a story that, just before he was finally taken up into unity with the divine element, the Buddha chose to return to the world that had not yet been liberated, in order to help those of his brothers who had not yet reached fulfilment. As long as there are still unredeemed people, who have not yet been liberated, genuine mystics, both in the East and in the West, refuse to possess perfect happiness.

O. *Does mysticism mean something different for you from faith itself? When people talk about mysticism, after all, it often seems as though they are talking about an extra, something that is additional to the ordinary experience of faith.*

S. I don't accept that it is just an extra. Mysticism is at the very heart of faith. It is the growth, the dynamic growth of faith. It certainly was that in the case of John of the Cross. Insofar as the Jesuits have ever been concerned with mysticism, they have always regarded it as exceptional and they have usually emphasized the secondary phenomena that accompany it. Thomas Aquinas insisted that those epiphenomena did not touch the centre of mysticism, but could be traced back to psychosomatic aspects. The Jesuit mystical writers have dissociated mysticism from faith and described it as an exceptional experience of God. I wonder whether that way of talking is really in accordance with the teaching of Ignatius Loyola.

Our mystical relationship with the one whom we, following Jesus' example, call 'our Father' ought to inspire us to do justice. Mysticism and solidarity with the poor form a single whole! Mysticism on its own, without any socio-political consequences, can come to nothing.

13
'I am not writing for posterity'

O. *Are you afraid of getting older?*

S. Yes. I am not afraid of dying, but I am afraid of getting older. I am not conscious of getting older at present, but I can't help noticing others, especially in this community here, being taken around in a wheelchair, for example. Sometimes the thought occurs to me — perhaps in five or six years' time someone will be pushing me around in a wheelchair and I'll be completely dependent on other people. A burden to others.

I would hate to end up in an old people's home. Mainly because I would hate not to be among young people, people with vitality. I really must have young people around me. If I don't, I find that my mind atrophies. Perhaps, when I am really old and broken, I will be able to join a community with older and younger members, where I am still able to do something. As long as I can retain some inner vitality myself, there will be some hope, I think. The worst thing for me would undoubtedly be if I could no longer go along with younger people — if I became reactionary!

O. *What would you do if you became conscious of becoming reactionary?*

S. I think I would try to remain silent and make room for others.

O. *Supposing you did become a burden to others and were unable to add anything positive to your life — would you consider euthanasia?*

S. No, not for myself. I might be able to justify it for others, but I wouldn't accept euthanasia for myself. That is certain. In fact, I would tell the doctor: Don't use any technical devices and aids on me. Don't use any apparatus on my body just to extend my life. But just to say it has all become so bad and your mind is so clouded and so on that all you need to do is to take a pill or something like that — no, I wouldn't do it. Well, that's what I think at present. No, I wouldn't accept euthanasia for myself.

O. *Your health is still good, isn't it? You may be able to go on writing for another ten or more years.*

S. Yes, I hope so.

O. *What do you plan to write?*

S. I want to continue my study of hermeneutics. A book of about five or six hundred pages, outlining my method. It will, of course, be a very academic book, dealing with structuralism, the materialistic method of interpreting Scripture and so on. I think it ought to be an important book not only for theologians and philosophers, but also for those who specialize in literature. And I would also like to write an eschatology. I have done one already, a long time ago, when I was at Louvain. I would have to rewrite it completely. I would also like to rewrite my first great book, the *Sacramentele heilseconomie*, which was published in 1952. I would rewrite it from an entirely different point of departure and would follow a completely new approach. When I wrote it more than thirty years ago, my approach was far too sacral. But it would take a lot of work and I just don't know whether I shall be able to undertake all that research in early texts when I am five years older. I think I would also like to write a very ordinary book, as simple and as well written as possible, outlining Christianity in a personal, concrete and objective way, from my own standpoint, of course. What does Jesus mean? I would try to answer that question and speak if I had something to say and be silent if I had nothing more to say.

O. *Do you often meet your readers? Do you have any feed-back about your books?*

S. Yes, I have met people who have read my books at conferences here and abroad. I also get a lot of letters and now especially from the United States, from people who are quite unknown to me. They are always thanking me for what they call the 'grace of my book'! I get a few letters, but only a few, from people who damn me as the incarnation of pride, as Satan personified — the false teacher who wants to destroy the Church but is too much of a coward to leave it. It amazes me how strict orthodoxy so often leads to an unloving and unChristian attitude.

Many lay people read my books too. I have had letters from them saying they have taken as much as two years to read and study one of my volumes. Others, of course, buy the books but don't read them. They are often used for sermons. My second great book, *Christ*, is apparently used in this way more than the others.

O. *What effect will your work have, do you think?*

S. The results of my work I will leave, I think, to history. I am not writing for posterity. I am writing for people here and now. In ten year's time, perhaps, another approach will be needed.

O. *You dedicated your* Jesus *book to all readers, those whom you knew and those whom you did not know and especially to Cardinal Alfrink.*

S. Yes, because I am very grateful to him. He invited me to take part as an expert in the Second Vatican Council. He trusted me completely as a theologian and defended me when I had my first difficulties with Rome in 1968.

O. *What part did he play, do you think, in the recent history of the Dutch Church? Should be, in your opinion, have resisted the Vatican more firmly, for example, in the appointment of Bishops Simononis and Gijsen?*

S. I am still quite convinced that he guided the Dutch Church in a quite excellent way during a most difficult period. Even when he did not agree with everything that was happening in the community of believers here, he nonetheless gave complete confidence to those believers. It is, of course, possible to disagree as to whether he should have left things in a state of submissive regret after all that happened in connection with Bishop Moors' successor in the diocese of Limburg. Parishes and even families are still divided by unresolved disputes there and a great deal is still suppressed. The problems and sufferings in Bishop Gijsen's part of the Netherlands are, you might say, the unpaid bills of the Church.

O. *You have mentioned the Second Vatican Council several times in the course of our conversation. Was it a very important event in your life, would you say?*

S. The Council was very significant for me. Or rather, the period I spent in Rome during the Council, since I never entered the debating chamber during the assemblies of the Council itself, because I was not an 'official' expert. No, it was a great experience for me because for the first time in my life I met theologians whose work I had previously read and there was very soon a close bond of friendship between us. I also got to know many Bishops. They were going around with their pastoral problems and I remember it being said they were 'without a shepherd or a guide'. My immediate concern was to edit the fundamental version of the chapter on 'Marriage and the Family' in the conciliar document on the Church in the Modern World (*Gaudium et spes*). I composed this together with Professor Victor Heylen and Bishop Heuschen.

Most of my work consisted of giving lectures to the most heterogeneous groups of bishops, sometimes as many as two hundred of them at the same time. These lectures usually dealt with themes that I approved or disapproved of in the conciliar schemas. I may in that way have been able to influence the bishops indirectly in their acceptance or rejection of conciliar texts.

At the beginning of the Council, no papers were read in addition to the pre-conciliar schemas in which criticism was expressed. Mine was, I believe, the only paper — a stencilled text of about sixty pages that Mgr Bekkers, the leader of the Dutch Church at the time, had asked me to prepare. He had it translated into several different languages and at the beginning of the Council about two thousand copies of it were distributed to the bishops. As the Council progressed, the production of papers of this kind increased and it became very hard work!

For me, the Council was basically giving lectures to conferences of bishops — Dutch bishops, Polish bishops, Indian bishops and Brazilian bishops. The discussions that followed the lectures were especially interesting. I learned a great deal about the cultural framework within which the different bishops lived with their believers. Several times objections were raised by those 'in authority' to my lectures to the bishops. They could hardly forbid me to give the lectures, but it was announced once in the lecture-hall that 'these lectures' were not subject to the 'authority of the Council'. For all of us, the first session was a real battlefield and we were fighting for our survival. Would the pre-Vatican II ideas prevail or would those who held them prove to be in a minority?

O. *What was your experience of the climate in the Church in the nineteen-sixties? What really happened in those years after the Council? What has changed since then and what still remains?*

S. What struck me perhaps most of all when I came back from the Council was that our enthusiasm was not fully shared by those who stayed at home. Mgr Bekkers also experienced that as a cold shower. So he went on a tour of many of the towns in the Netherlands with one or other of his experts with the aim of interpreting and elucidating the meaning of the Council so that something would be conveyed of the living experience of Rome. Many people's enthusiasm had been shattered for good by the so-called 'black week' after the final session of the Council. (Paul VI intervened in such a way that a real limitation was placed on the collegiality of the bishops; he affirmed that, with or without the approval of the world's bishops, the pope was able to govern and lead the Catholic Church.)

I did what I could by writing and so on to prevent that 'black week' from poisoning the whole renewal movement in the Church and in fact many people continued to be enthusiastic for many years and there was some real renewal. Above all people were able to breathe more freely.

Because of an irony of history, only a few years after the Church had been urged by Vatican II ultimately to accept the modern age, 'modernity' itself was fiercely criticized by the world and the movement that we know as the criticism of society began to gain ground. In that sense, Vatican II was, compared with the great 'feudal' encyclicals of Leo XIII and his successors up to the time of Pius XII, the first great liberal, bourgeois council, in which the Church accepted for the first time the acquired rights and ideals of middle-class society — religious freedom, freedom of conscience, tolerance and ecumenism. And, ironically, that happened just at the time when the world was getting ready to criticize the misuse by the West of precisely those liberal values, to the great disadvantage of the poor and the Third World.

So, for this reason, the breakthrough achieved by the Second Vatican Council has never been able to become a full reality and at the same time the Church has been confronted with completely new problems, very few of which were even discussed at the Council. This accounts for the ambiguity of the Council, however positive its achievement may have been. The experience of the Council itself, rather than its texts, I would say, is what continues to be valid.

The nineteen-seventies were years in which we became very alarmed about our welfare. We began to criticize our own central position in Europe. Young people became uneasy and even alienated with regard to Vatican II and not primarily because of factors within the Church, but because the general climate of thought was changing so radically in Western society. The contrast with the early nineteen-sixties, when the Council took place, could not have been greater! The world at that time had just surmounted the chaos of the Second World War and had been made bold and confident by successful economic development and an international perspective of peace and prosperity. There are elements of this naive optimism to be found, for example, in the Pastoral Constitution of Vatican II, the Church in the Modern World, which speaks of the part that the Church has to play in this great development on the way to universal prosperity. But things have changed and, since the nineteen-seventies, we have surrendered.

The fundamental experience of the Second Vatican Council, which, as I have said, still remains valid, is not so much that the Church has to be adapted to the modern era, but rather that the real and lasting dimension of the Church is evangelical renewal. We have once again to learn how to listen to God and to the world and how to reject the certainties that have clung to the Church from its own past.

O. *Have you ever given religious instruction to children?*

S. Once, in America. It was in 1968 and the children were eleven or twelve years old. My nephew in the United States told me the sisters who taught at his school very much wanted me to speak to his class. I couldn't speak to children and certainly not in English! But my nephew persuaded me with an argument that I couldn't resist: 'The sisters think of you as we think of the Beatles'.

I can't remember whether I succeeded or not. I haven't made any notes of the experience! But I think it was very difficult. But, of course, it must be possible to speak to children about faith. I imagine the best way of approaching children is via the liturgy, by letting them take part. A good deal should become clear to them in that way.

Once I had to lead in the liturgy when an older member of my family had died. Father asked me to do something in the liturgy for the children and forget about the adults. My sisters talked to the little ones and asked them: 'What would you like to ask him about faith? He may be able to help you.' So they put their questions to me during the liturgy. It is incredible what they contributed to the experience!

O. *What kind of liturgy do you prefer?*

S. A politicized liturgy. But it doesn't have always to be so emphatically political, of course. The contemplative element is indispensable in the liturgy and faith must be proclaimed. And then the whole celebration must be a unity. What I always think is that prayer — and that is mysticism or I don't really know what it can be — without social commitment becomes reduced to mere sentimentality and commitment to society without prayer often becomes grim and even barbaric. I think what I would like to see most of all is a unity between mysticism and commitment, just as I would like to experience unity between quiet reflection and active commitment in politics.

O. *Do you speak to God?*

S. Yes.

O. *As a man speaks to his friend?*

S. Yes — and I have never found it difficult to do that. When I was younger, my speaking to God was, of course, different from what it is now. It happened much more as a matter of course. I had the confidence and serenity of a young Roman Catholic of the period. Later it became less automatic, but I still went on talking to God in that naive and ordinary way. If you don't talk to God first, you can't talk about him.

O. *Would you write a psalm to end this book with?*

S. Only if you make it a little more poetical.

O. *No, I won't do that. A psalm about your own life. Will you do that?*

S. Yes, I will.

O. *So now we will stop talking. We've been doing it for almost twenty hours!*

'DO NOT FEAR'

Are you a God at hand and not a God far off?	Jer 23:23
Truly, you are a hidden God.	Is 45:15
Or do you hide your face from us, to see what our end will be?	Deut 32:20
And yet you do not willingly afflict or grieve us.	Lam 3:33
You are ready to be sought by those who do not ask for you; you are ready to be found by those who do not seek you.	Is 65:1
Do I look for you in chaos?	Is 45:19c
I hear you saying, Lord: 'I, the Lord, speak salvation and declare what is right'.	Is 41:19d
But the poor and needy seek water and there is none and their tongues are parched with thirst.	Is 41:17

How can my soul wait in silence
for you, God, who are my salvation?   Ps 62:1

May you find people, Lord, who work for justice.   Is 64:5

Then we shall be able to say to everyone:
You are our God.
You set people free.
You have heard my cry.

You have heard me and said:
'Do not fear!'   Lam 3:37

'Behold, I am doing a new thing;
now it springs forth — do you not see it?'   Is 43:19

Lord, I believe;
help my unbelief!   Mk 9:24b

I am a poor fool, Lord —
teach me how to pray.   (Guido Gezelle)

Bibliography of Edward Schillebeeckx

(The following list contains only those books that have been published in English translation)

Christ the Sacrament of the Encounter with God (London and New York, 1963).

Mary, Mother of the Redemption (London and New York, 1964).

Marriage. Secular Reality and Saving Mystery, I and II (London and Melbourne, 1965).

Cardinal Alfrink (Notre Dame, 1965).

Revelation and Theology (London and Melbourne, 1967).

The Concept of Truth and Theological Renewal (London and Sydney, 1968).

The Eucharist (London and Sydney, 1968).

God and Man (London and Sydney, 1969).

God the Future of Man (London and Sydney, 1969).

World and Church (London and Sydney, 1971).

The Mission of the Church (London, 1973).

The Understanding of Faith. Interpretation and Criticism (London, 1974).

Jesus. An Experiment in Christology (London and New York, 1979).

Christ. The Christian Experience in the Modern World (London, 1980) = *Christ. The Experience of Jesus as Lord* (New York, 1980).

Jesus and Christ. Interim Report on the Books Jesus and Christ (London and New York, 1980).

Ministry. A Case for Change (London, 1981) = *Ministry. Leadership in the Community of Jesus Christ* (New York, 1981).

Question what you thought before

Continuum Impacts - books that change the way we think

Continuum Impacts
CHANGING MINDS

www.continuumbooks.com